MW00655624

CHRIST-CENTERED

Exposition

NT / COMMENTARY

AUTHOR **Daniel L. Akin**

SERIES EDITORS **David Platt, Daniel L. Akin, and Tony Merida**

CHRIST-CENTERED
Exposition

EXALTING JESUS IN

1, 2, & 3 JOHN

HOLMAN
REFERENCE
BRENTWOOD, TENNESSEE

SERIES DEDICATION

Dedicated to Adrian Rogers and John Piper. They have taught us to love the gospel of Jesus Christ, to preach the Bible as the inerrant Word of God, to pastor the Church for which our Savior died, and to have a passion to see all nations gladly worship the Lamb.

—David Platt, Tony Merida, and Danny Akin
March 2013

TABLE OF CONTENTS

ACKNOWLEDGMENTS

I would like to thank Shane Shaddix, Mary Jo Haselton, Kim Humphrey, and Amy Whitfield, each of whom made significant contributions to this volume. You all have blessed and enriched my life.

Daniel L. Akin

SERIES INTRODUCTION

Augustine said, "Where Scripture speaks, God speaks." The editors of the Christ-Centered Exposition Commentary series believe that where God speaks, the pastor must speak. God speaks through His written Word. We must speak from that Word. We believe the Bible is God breathed, authoritative, inerrant, sufficient, understandable, necessary, and timeless. We also affirm that the Bible is a Christ-centered book; that is, it contains a unified story of redemptive history of which Jesus is the hero. Because of this Christ-centered trajectory that runs from Genesis 1 through Revelation 22, we believe the Bible has a corresponding global-missions thrust. From beginning to end, we see God's mission as one of making worshipers of Christ from every tribe and tongue worked out through this redemptive drama in Scripture. To that end we must preach the Word.

In addition to these distinct convictions, the Christ-Centered Exposition Commentary series has some distinguishing characteristics. First, this series seeks to display exegetical accuracy. What the Bible says is what we want to say. While not every volume in the series will be a verse-by-verse commentary, we nevertheless desire to handle the text carefully and explain it rightly. Those who teach and preach bear the heavy responsibility of saying what God has said in His Word and declaring what God has done in Christ. We desire to handle God's Word faithfully, knowing that we must give an account for how we have fulfilled this holy calling (Jas 3:1).

Second, the Christ-Centered Exposition Commentary series has pastors in view. While we hope others will read this series, such as parents, teachers, small-group leaders, and student ministers, we desire to provide a commentary busy pastors will use for weekly preparation of biblically faithful and gospel-saturated sermons. This series is not academic in nature. Our aim is to present a readable and pastoral style of commentaries. We believe this aim will serve the church of the Lord Jesus Christ.

Third, we want the Christ-Centered Exposition Commentary series to be known for the inclusion of helpful illustrations and theologically driven applications. Many commentaries offer no help in illustrations, and few offer any kind of help in application. Often those that do offer illustrative material and application unfortunately give little serious attention to the text. While giving ourselves primarily to explanation, we also hope to serve readers by providing inspiring and illuminating illustrations coupled with timely and timeless application.

Finally, as the name suggests, the editors seek to exalt Jesus from every book of the Bible. In saying this, we are not commending wild allegory or fanciful typology. We certainly believe we must be constrained to the meaning intended by the divine Author Himself, the Holy Spirit of God. However, we also believe the Bible has a messianic focus, and our hope is that the individual authors will exalt Christ from particular texts. Luke 24:25-27,44-47 and John 5:39,46 inform both our hermeneutics and our homiletics. Not every author will do this the same way or have the same degree of Christ-centered emphasis. That is fine with us. We believe faithful exposition that is Christ centered is not monolithic. We do believe, however, that we must read the whole Bible as Christian Scripture. Therefore, our aim is both to honor the historical particularity of each biblical passage and to highlight its intrinsic connection to the Redeemer.

The editors are indebted to the contributors of each volume. The reader will detect a unique style from each writer, and we celebrate these unique gifts and traits. While distinctive in approach, the authors share a common characteristic in that they are pastoral theologians. They love the church, and they regularly preach and teach God's Word to God's people. Further, many of these contributors are younger voices. We think these new, fresh voices can serve the church well, especially among a rising generation that has the task of proclaiming the Word of Christ and the Christ of the Word to the lost world.

We hope and pray this series will serve the body of Christ well in these ways until our Savior returns in glory. If it does, we will have succeeded in our assignment.

David Platt
Daniel L. Akin
Tony Merida
Series Editors
February 2013

1, 2, & 3 John

A Life Like No Other: Jesus the Incarnate Word

1 JOHN 1:1-4

Main Idea: Jesus Christ is the God-man who is the one basis of true Christian fellowship and eternal life.

I. **Have a Passion to Know This Life (1:1-2).**
   A. He is divine.
   B. He is human.
II. **Have a Passion to Share This Life (1:3).**
   A. We want to invite everyone into our fellowship.
   B. We want to invite everyone into our family.
III. **Have a Passion to Enjoy This Life (1:4).**
   A. Promote joy that is full (1:4).
   B. Press on in holiness (2:1).
   C. Pursue correct doctrine (2:26).
   D. Provide assurance of salvation (5:13).

Christianity stands or falls on the person and work of Jesus Christ. It succeeds or fails on whether or not a true and genuine incarnation actually took place in space and time. The options as to who Jesus is and what Jesus did can basically be reduced to four. He could have been a *liar*—someone who simply was not who he claimed to be and knew it. He could have been a *lunatic*—someone who thought he was somebody, but in fact he was not. He could have been a *legend*—someone who was not who others later imagined him to be. Or He could be the *Lord*—He is who He said He is, and His birth, life, death, and resurrection prove it to be true.[1]

In our twenty-first-century context, we constantly face confusion, distortions, inaccuracies, and outright denials of the Jesus revealed in the Bible. This is nothing new. The apostle John faced the same challenges in the first century, and he penned 1 John to set the record straight. He knew that it was absolutely essential to get the "Jesus question" right!

---

[1] This dilemma is posed in C. S. Lewis's *Mere Christianity* (pp. 54–56) among other places.

John, the son of Zebedee and brother of James (the first apostle to be martyred, cf. Acts 12:2), wrote five books of the New Testament. He wrote the Gospel of John to *convert sinners*. He wrote the epistles of John to *confirm the saints*. And he wrote the book of Revelation to *coronate the Savior*.

John is a wonderful author who always gives us his purpose for writing. In his Gospel the key is located at the end, in John 20:31, where he writes, "But these are written so that you may believe Jesus is the Messiah, the Son of God, and by believing you may have life in His name." In Revelation the key is deposited at the front, in Revelation 1:19, where he quotes Jesus: "Therefore write what you have seen, what is, and what will take place after this." In 1 John, however, there are four keys that are scattered throughout the five chapters and 105 verses that help us unlock this much-beloved letter. In 1 John 1:4, John says he wrote *to promote full joy* in the family of God. In 2:1 he says he wrote *to prevent sin* in the family of God. In 2:26 he says he wrote *to protect from false teachers* in the family of God. And in 5:13 he says his purpose was *to provide assurance of salvation* in the family of God.

In this book—written from Ephesus sometime between AD 80 and 95, most likely to churches in Asia Minor (modern Turkey)—three important themes are linked to the four purposes that open the doors to the wonderful truths we discover in this letter: (1) right belief in Jesus; (2) right obedience to God's commands; and (3) right love for one another. These themes provide "avenues of assurance," whereby I can know that I am a Christian. Similar to how the Gospel of John was written that we might *have* eternal life (John 20:31), 1 John was written that we might *know* we have eternal life. By repeatedly applying these avenues of assurance, John will expose those who profess Christ but do not know Him, and he will assure those who know Christ but may have doubts about their salvation. In other words, it is possible to know Christ and have doubts. It is also possible to profess Christ and be a liar.

There is great timelessness to the truths we will encounter in this letter that are true anywhere, anytime, and under any circumstances. They are truths for the community of faith that confesses Jesus as Lord, keeps the commands of the Father, and loves one another. John begins in this prologue by putting before us three great truths about the life of Jesus. In so doing he says, "Look! Here is a life like no other!"

Have a Passion to Know This Life
1 JOHN 1:1-2

First John 1:1-4 constitutes the introduction to this General Epistle. These verses make up one of the four great beginnings in the Bible. Genesis 1:1 recounts the beginning of creation. Mark 1:1 tells of the beginning of the gospel of Jesus Christ, the Son of God. John 1:1 reveals the Word who is God and was there in the beginning. And here, in 1 John 1:1, John reveals the incarnate Son, who became a man in the person of Jesus of Nazareth.

John wants us to know, and know rightly, this "Word of life" who invaded space and time and who makes it possible for us to have fellowship and eternal intimacy with the one true God (v. 3). He draws attention to two important truths concerning this life, the life of Jesus, which is like no other.

He Is Divine

The Son Jesus Christ (v. 3) is "what was from the beginning" (v. 1) and is "the eternal life that was with the Father" (v. 2). Jesus Christ, who is the Father's Son (v. 3), has always eternally existed with the Father as God. There has never been a time when the Son was not. Never. He was before the beginning, in the beginning, and from the beginning. This is what John believed. This is what Jesus taught. Jesus Himself boldly declared in John 8:58, "Before Abraham was, I am" (indicating He is the God of Exod 3:14). In John 10:30 He said, "The Father and I are one." And in John 14:9 He told Philip, "The one who has seen Me has seen the Father." Clearly Jesus believed Himself to be God, and John confessed the same. This life is the life of undiminished deity made flesh in Jesus of Nazareth. There never was a time when the Son was not, and there will never be a time when He will not be.

He Is Human

John now, as an apostle and friend of Jesus, presents a rigorous defense of the real and genuine humanity of the Son. John speaks as one who was an eyewitness of all that Jesus said and did. This is neither hearsay nor a secondhand account. The apostle presents an eyewitness account of what John Piper has called "the stumbling block of the incarnation" ("Eternal Life"). John says four things concerning this "Word of life": (1) We heard Him with our ears. John repeats this in verse 3 for emphasis. (2) We saw Him with our eyes. John states this three times for emphasis in the first three verses. Furthermore, "we have observed" Him. There was an intentional, intense, and continuous gazing at and contemplation of this man named Jesus. For three years we watched and observed His every move. (3) We touched Him with our hands. He was a real flesh-and-blood human being. He was no ghost or phantom. (4) We testify and declare (both present tense), as *bona fide* eyewitnesses, this "eternal life that was with the Father and was revealed to us." Notice again how John uses repetition. Twice he says the eternal life was manifested to us in Jesus Christ. He presents for anyone to consider an audible, visible, and tangible witness concerning Jesus, the Word of life, the eternal life.

Let me make both a historical and a theological observation at this point. Historically, John was countering an early form of what is called "Gnosticism," a term based on the Greek word that means knowledge. Gnostics appeared in a number of varieties, but they all had two basic convictions in common. First, they believed that matter is evil (or at least inferior to spiritual realities). Second, they believed that salvation is by a mystical, even secretive, knowledge. This bred extreme arrogance and pride among the Gnostic factions, and it led them to deny with great fervency a true and genuine incarnation of the Christ. One camp, called "Docetists" (from the Gk *dokein*, meaning "to appear"), claimed Jesus was a ghost or phantom—He only *appeared* to be human. Another camp, led by a man named Cerinthus, said the Christ-spirit came on and empowered the man Jesus at His baptism, but it also left Him at the cross. John deals with the Docetists here in 1:1-4. He will take on Cerinthus in 5:6-12.

Theologically, it is imperative that we understand the essential nature of the doctrine of the incarnation. The biblical Jesus is no myth, fairy tale, or fable. He is no ghost or illusion. He is indeed the God who took on full humanity. "The Word became flesh," says John (John 1:14). And Jesus Christ is fully God and fully man. He is not half God and half man, all God and no man, or all man and no God. Nor is He simply a man uniquely in touch with the divine. No, He is the God-man, like no one else who will ever live. He has always been with the Father, and at Bethlehem He came to be with us. This is the scandal, the stumbling block of the incarnation. Piper says it so very well:

Many are willing to believe in Christ if he remains a merely spiritual reality. But when we preach that Christ has become a particular man in a particular place issuing particular commands and dying on a particular cross exposing the particular sins of our particular lives, then the preaching ceases to be acceptable for many.

I don't think it is so much the mystery of a divine and human nature in one person that causes most people to stumble over the doctrine of the incarnation. The stumbling block is that if the doctrine is true, every single person in the world must obey this one particular Jewish man. Everything he says is law. Everything he did is perfect. And the particularity of his work and word flow out into history in the form of a particular inspired book (written in the particular languages of Greek and Hebrew) that claims a universal authority over every other book that has ever been written.

This is the stumbling block of the incarnation—when God becomes a man, he strips away every pretense of man to be God. We can no longer do our own thing; we must do what this one Jewish man wants us to do. We can no longer pose as self-sufficient, because this one Jewish man says we are all sick with sin and must come to him for healing. We can no longer depend on our own wisdom to find life, because this one Jewish man who lived for 30 obscure years in a little country in the Middle East says, "I am the way, the truth, and the life."

When God becomes a man, man ceases to be the measure of all things, and this man becomes the measure of all things. This is simply intolerable to the rebellious heart of men and women. The incarnation is a violation of the bill of human rights written by Adam and Eve in the Garden of Eden. It is totalitarian. It's authoritarian! Imperialism! Despotism! Usurpation! Absolutism! Who does he think he is!

GOD! (Piper, "Eternal Life")

Benjamin Franklin perfectly exhibits this aversion to the historical reality of the God-man. In a letter dated March 9, 1790, Franklin said,

As to Jesus of Nazareth . . . I think the system of morals and his religion, as he left them to us, the best the world ever saw or is likely to see; but I apprehend it has received various corrupting changes, and I have, with most of the present dissenters in England, some doubts as to his divinity; tho' it is a question I do not dogmatize upon, having never studied it, and think it needless to busy myself with it now. (Franklin, "Letter to Ezra Stiles")

On the contrary, it is never needless to busy ourselves with Jesus. If He is who He claimed to be, that identity changes everything. We should all have a passion to know this life.

Have a Passion to Share This Life
1 JOHN 1:3

The impact that Jesus has on His followers cannot be put into words. They were radically changed and really did "turn the world upside down" (Acts 17:6). The impact of the life of Jesus, this "life like no other," compelled them to take Him and His gospel to the nations. They simply believed they must. They had no choice. What they had experienced in Jesus they wanted others to experience too.

We Want to Invite Everyone into Our Fellowship

Verse 3 begins with the phrase "what we have seen and heard." As we noted earlier, "seeing" is highlighted in each of the first three verses. Interestingly, the main verb of the prologue does not appear until now. It is the word "declare." It means to "proclaim" (ESV) or "announce" (GNT, NET). John says we cannot remain silent about this eternal life-giving Word. What we have heard, seen, looked upon, and touched we must share with others. We will testify and bear witness concerning Jesus Christ, and we will proclaim the gospel of Jesus Christ.

To what end? "So that you may have fellowship along with us." John speaks of fellowship four times in this letter, all in 1:3-7. The Greek word is *koinonia*, and it speaks of sharing in common something that is significant and important. It entails the joy and oneness in a group of people who are in accord regarding something that really matters. You share common values, beliefs, and goals. You love the same things. You pursue a common agenda.

John so loves the church, the believing community of faith in Jesus, that he wants to invite everyone to become a part. No one is to be excluded from this invitation. No one who comes by the way of Jesus—the Word who gives life, eternal life, a life of both quality and quantity—will be denied entrance. The moment you enter into a personal relationship with Him, this life is yours. And this fellowship is yours as well.

We Want to Invite Everyone into Our Family

The fellowship that exists among followers of Jesus is far richer and deeper than that of a college fraternity or sorority. It is far richer and deeper than that of a favorite sports team or community club. It is far richer and deeper than even that of national identity or ethnic heritage. It is the "fellowship of family" that transcends any and all artificial barriers that have afflicted the human race since the fall. By means of the incarnation and His perfect atoning sacrifice (2:2), we are now a "fellowship family" with the Father and with His Son Jesus Christ. When Jesus becomes our Savior, God becomes our Father. It is a package deal. Later, in 2:23, John will write, "No one who denies the Son can have the Father; he who confesses the Son has the Father as well."

Unlike every other religion in the world, Christianity brings us into intimate relationship with a God who is Savior and Father. And He is a perfect Savior and a perfect heavenly Father. In addition, you get a whole bunch of brothers and sisters thrown in as well "from every nation, tribe, people, and language" (Rev 7:9). We Christians must never forget that we have more in common with a Chinese Christian, an African sister, and a brother in South America than a next-door neighbor who does not know Christ. And never forget that this eternal life that has transformed us is the eternal life we must proclaim to our neighbor here and among the nations in order that they might become family. We continually want to add more!

Have a Passion to Enjoy This Life
1 JOHN 1:4

God is glorified in us when we find our joy in Him. A common theology, a common Savior, a common Father, and a common experience of joy unites all who have come to know this life that is like no other, life in Jesus the incarnate Word. These common blessings are woven into a beautiful tapestry throughout 1 John, and they are highlighted by the four keys we noted earlier, keys that he introduces by saying that he is writing or has written "these things." How might we enjoy these blessings?

Promote Joy That Is Full (1 John 1:4)

John wrote this letter "so that our joy may be complete." Not partial, but complete. Full. All we could want or ever need. John is echoing the words he heard from Jesus: "I have spoken these things to you so that My joy may be in you and your joy may be complete" (John 15:11); and "Until now you have asked for nothing in My name. Ask and you will receive, so that your joy may be complete" (John 16:24). We have a fullness of joy in our shared life with Jesus. That fullness of joy is ours through our friendship with one another and with God, who is now our Father. And all of it made possible by the gospel of Jesus Christ, God's Son.

Press On in Holiness (1 John 2:1)

Christians never become sinless in their time on earth, but they should sin less as they enjoy their new life in Christ. This striving to be more and more like Jesus (and note the amazing promise in 3:2!) is a life of joy lived not out of obligation, but gratitude—gospel gratitude, because Jesus died the death we should have died (2:2) and He lived the life we should have lived (2:6). This life of holiness is marked particularly by joy, by keeping Christ's commands (2:3), and by loving one another (2:10).

Pursue Correct Doctrine (1 John 2:26)

When John writes a letter to help us enjoy Jesus, the Word of life, he fills it with theology. This theology is *doctrinal* and it is *practical*. It is also *pastoral*. Thus he warns us concerning those who would deceive us with false doctrine—those he marks in the most striking manner with the designation "antichrists" (2:18,22; 4:3; 2 John 7).

John believes theology matters and so should we. Our joy—which is made complete in fellowship with the Father, His Son Jesus Christ, and one another—is grounded in a shared theology. To enjoy this life we must believe the theology about this Word of life. There can be no cafeteria approach to Jesus Christ, where we pick what we like and leave what we don't. John had no interest in a "Jesus minus theology" or a "Jesus plus theology." Thabiti Anyabwile says it like this:

> To receive the Word of life is to embrace Jesus as He offers Himself in the gospel. That phrase—"as He offers himself in the gospel"—is very important. We must receive Jesus—the

Word of life, the eternal life, the Son of God—not as we imagine Him to be, or as we like to think of Him, or as someone else believes Him to be. We do not truly receive Jesus if we do not accept Him as He defines Himself.

We know that we are Christians and have received God's salvation when we humbly accept the Word of life, which means to believe in Jesus Christ, the Son of God, who appeared in our flesh, was crucified to take our punishment for our sin, was raised from the grave three days later for our justification with God, and is coming again to bring the fullness of God's kingdom. Is that the Jesus you have received? (unpublished sermon manuscript)

Provide Assurance of Salvation (1 John 5:13)

John knew it was possible to be saved and doubt. Those who deny this must deny 1 John 5:13. I believe he also knew that doubt will discourage us, cause us to fear and lose confidence, and negatively impact our joy. So he wrote these five chapters to provide assurance that we are in the family because we have believed and trusted in Jesus the Son of God. Anyone who says, "If you are 99-percent certain you are saved you are 100-percent lost!" is teaching false doctrine, at least concerning this important theological truth. Still, John does not want us to wonder if we are saved. He wants us to have assurance that we are saved. First and foremost, we must look to Christ and believe. We must look to the cross and trust. Then we must examine our obedience and our affections. These avenues of assurance are found on every corner in 1 John.

Conclusion

In AD 325 church leaders from around the Roman Empire gathered in Nicea (in modern day Turkey). The issue on the table was "Who is the Son?" A popular Presbyter from Alexandria named Arius said, "God became a Father, and the Son was not always; . . . once He was not; . . . He was created" ("Athanasius: Select Works and Letters" in Schaff). Two men, Alexander and Athanasius, strongly opposed this view, believing that biblical truth and the doctrine of salvation itself hung in the balance. In God's providence the Arians were defeated, and what we know as "The Nicene Creed" was set forth as the biblical and orthodox understanding of the nature and person of Jesus. Both His humanity and His

deity are beautifully affirmed. And His person and work as the Christ
are wonderfully balanced. In glad confession and worship, may we also
confess with our spiritual fathers that this too we believe!

The Nicene Creed

I believe in one God, the Father Almighty, Maker of heaven
and earth, and of all things visible and invisible.

And in one Lord Jesus Christ, the only-begotten Son of
God, begotten of the Father before all worlds; God of God,
Light of Light, very God of very God; begotten, not made,
being of one substance with the Father, by whom all things
were made.

Who, for us men and for our salvation, came down from
heaven, and was incarnate by the Holy Spirit of the virgin
Mary, and was made man; and was crucified also for us under
Pontius Pilate; He suffered and was buried; and the third day
He rose again, according to the Scriptures; and ascended
into heaven, and sits on the right hand of the Father; and He
shall come again, with glory, to judge the quick and the dead;
whose kingdom shall have no end.

And I believe in the Holy Ghost, the Lord and Giver of
Life; who proceeds from the Father and the Son; who with the
Father and the Son together is worshipped and glorified; who
spoke by the prophets.

And I believe in one holy catholic and apostolic Church.
I acknowledge one baptism for the remission of sins; and I
look for the resurrection of the dead, and the life of the world
to come. Amen. (https://www.ccel.org/creeds/nicene.creed
.html, accessed Feb. 11, 2014)

Reflect and Discuss

1. How are the person and work of Jesus central to Christianity? What
   alternative ideas have you heard someone propose about the heart
   of Christianity?
2. Read through the book of 1 John. Where do you see the themes of
   right belief about Jesus, right obedience to God's commands, and
   right love for one another?

3. Why does John emphasize both Jesus' humanity and His deity at the beginning of this letter? How might we go astray if we do not affirm both truths?
4. How is the doctrine of the incarnation offensive or threatening to those who have not understood and embraced the gospel?
5. How does an encounter with Jesus fuel missions?
6. Why does John want others to share in the knowledge of Christ? How can we grow to experience the same motives?
7. How is Christian fellowship similar to and different from simple friendship?
8. Some theologians maintain that the very purpose of life is to experience and express joy in a relationship with God. Do you agree? What does it mean for joy to be "complete"?
9. When you think of holiness, do you see it as a burdensome obligation or as a blessing and a joy? How is holiness often misunderstood?
10. Why is assurance important for the believer? What are the grounds of our assurance?

Let God Be True and Every Man a Liar: A Mandate for Global Evangelization

1 JOHN 1:5–2:2

Main Idea: Jesus is our atonement and our advocate who reconciles us to God and sends us out to share the gospel message with the world.

I. **The World Must Know What God Says about Himself (1:5).**
   A. We have a gospel message to announce.
   B. We have a basic truth to affirm.
II. **The World Must Know What God Says about Sin (1:6-10).**
   A. Do not lie to others (1:6-7).
   B. Do not lie to yourself (1:8-9).
   C. Do not lie about God (1:10).
III. **The World Must Know What God Says about Jesus (2:1-2).**
   A. Jesus is our advocate (2:1).
   B. Jesus is our atonement (2:2).

Why does the world need a Savior? Why do we need an advocate (2:1)? Why must there be a propitiation (2:2)? The answer is sin. Humanity has a sin problem. It is our most fundamental problem, and it affects everyone. Of course, not everyone agrees with this assertion. In 1973 psychologist Karl Menninger shocked modern sensibilities with his book entitled *Whatever Became of Sin?* Sin? What a quaint and outdated idea. In this book Menninger provided a scathing critique of modern-day preaching and the noticeable absence of the "S" word: "sin." In a chapter titled, "The Disappearances of Sin: An Eyewitness Account," Menninger wrote,

> In all of the laments and reproaches made by our seers and
> prophets, one misses any mention of "sin," a word which used
> to be a veritable watchword of prophets. It was a word once
> in everyone's mind, but now rarely if ever heard. Does that
> mean that no sin is involved in all our troubles—sin with an
> "I" in the middle? Is no one any longer guilty of anything?
> Guilty perhaps of a sin that could be repented and repaired
> or atoned for? Is it only that someone may be stupid or sick or

criminal—or asleep? Wrong things are being done, we know; tares are being sown in the wheat field at night. But is no one responsible, no one answerable for these acts? Anxiety and depression we all acknowledge, and even vague guilt feelings; but has no one committed any sins? Where, indeed, did sin go? What became of it? (*Whatever Became of Sin?*, 13)

Menninger went on to explain,

> The very word "sin," which seems to have disappeared, was a proud word. It was once a strong word, an ominous and serious word. It described a central point in every civilized human being's life plan and life style. But the word went away. It has almost disappeared—the word, along with the notion. Why? Doesn't anyone sin anymore? Doesn't anyone believe in sin? (Ibid., 14)

He then asserts that what is new about our aversion to talking about sin is really the words we use to talk about it:

> It is surely nothing new that men want to get away from acknowledging their sins or even thinking about them. Is this not the religious history of mankind? Perhaps we are only more glib nowadays and equipped with more euphemisms. We can speak of error and transgression and infraction and mistakes without the naïve exposure that goes with serious use of that old-fashioned pietistic word "sin." (Ibid., 24)

Obviously sin is not a popular subject in our day. People will go to great lengths to hide it, rationalize it, or deny it. But we must understand that when they deny their sin they call God a liar. They challenge His Word and question His character. They say sin is not serious and Jesus did not need to die. They fall in line with liberal feminist theologian Delores Williams (formerly of Union Theological Seminary in New York), who once said, "I don't think we need a theory of atonement at all. I think Jesus came to show us something about life. . . . I don't think we need people hanging on crosses and blood dripping and weird stuff" (Deloris Williams, "Re-Imagining Jesus," 1:3–2). In one sense she is right: if we have no sin then we have no need of a Savior.

The apostle John has an altogether different understanding both of sin's severity and a Savior's necessity. He recognized the danger of calling God a liar and warns his "little children" (2:1) to be on alert.

Find out what a person believes about Jesus and what he thinks about
sin, John says. It will tell you a lot.

First John 1:5 is the basis for 1:6–2:2 and the foundation for 1:6–3:10,
the first half of John's letter. First John 1:5–3:10 emphasizes the truth
that God is light. The second half of the letter, 3:11–5:12, emphasizes
the truth that God is love. Following his declaration in verse 5 that "God
is light," John will weave together six "if" clauses and three "if we say"
statements (1:6,8,10) in 1:6–2:2. Nine times he will use the word "sin,"
and two times he will use the word "darkness." To think correctly about
Jesus, you must think correctly about sin. When you see sin for what it is
you will immediately see your need—the world's need—for Jesus as your
advocate (2:1) and your "atoning sacrifice" (2:2 NIV). You will also avoid
the error of calling God a liar.

The World Must Know What God Says about Himself
1 JOHN 1:5

The *New English Translation* renders verse 5 this way: "Now this is the
gospel message we have heard from him." This translation captures, I
believe, the heart of what John wants us to understand. We have a gospel, a "good news" message that the world needs. This message concerns Jesus Christ, who is identified as "what was from the beginning"
(1:1), "the Word of life" (1:1), "the eternal life" (1:2), the Father's Son
(1:3), the source of fellowship (1:3), and the source of joy (1:4). This is
God's witness concerning His Son and our Savior. This is what He thinks
about Jesus Christ. Having met this Savior in repentance and faith, we
have a divine assignment that involves the proclamation of a specific
gospel with a universal scope (2:2). This message is for the whole world.

We Have a Gospel Message to Announce

This gospel message is "what we have heard," and the perfect tense of
the verb means this message is still ringing in our ears. Further, it is a
message we heard from Him, from Jesus Himself. And it is a gospel message we continually "declare" to others. This message is one that has not
changed and will never change. There is an abiding and permanent
quality to this gospel. There also is an abiding and permanent mandate
to get it to the nations, to all 16,500 people groups in the world, with
6,900 still unreached (JoshuaProject.net, accessed Feb. 10, 2014).

That "God is light" is an embedded aspect of faithful gospel proclamation. It highlights the contrast between who God is and who we are without Him. The word "light" occurs in some form over 275 times in the Bible (95 times in the New Testament). It is a popular theme throughout the Scriptures.

The LORD is my light and my salvation—whom should I fear?
The LORD is the stronghold of my life—of whom should I be afraid?
(Ps 27:1)

For with You is life's fountain. In Your light we will see light.
(Ps 36:9)

Arise, shine, for your light has come, and the glory of the LORD shines over you. (Isa 60:1)

Nations will come to your light, and kings to the brightness of your radiance. (Isa 60:3)

The sun will no longer be your light by day, and the brightness of the moon will not shine on you; but the LORD will be your everlasting light, and your God will be your splendor. Your sun will no longer set, and your moon will not fade; for the LORD will be your everlasting light, and the days of your sorrow will be over. (Isa 60:19-20)

Do not rejoice over me, my enemy! Though I have fallen, I will stand up; though I sit in darkness, the LORD will be my light. (Mic 7:8)

The true light, who gives light to everyone, was coming into the world. (John 1:9)

Then Jesus spoke to them again: "I am the light of the world. Anyone who follows Me will never walk in the darkness but will have the light of life." (John 8:12)

"While you have the light, believe in the light so that you may become sons of light." Jesus said this, then went away and hid from them. (John 12:36)

I have come as a light into the world, so that everyone who believes in Me would not remain in darkness. (John 12:46)

God who is light and gives life has come to us as the light of the world in His Son Jesus Christ. The apostles saw this and they proclaimed it for all the world to hear. As Isaiah said, "The people walking in darkness have seen a great light; a light has dawned on those living in the land of darkness" (Isa 9:2).

We Have a Basic Truth to Affirm

An essential component of faithful gospel proclamation is an understanding of the nature and character of God. This is a theme that John will raise several times. For example, he teaches us that God is light (1:5), God is love (4:8,16), and God is true (5:20). Here he writes, "God is light and there is not darkness in Him—none" (author's translation). The double negative is used to emphasize this truth. For us a double negative is bad grammar. However, it is excellent theology. As we just saw, the image of light appears often in the Bible in reference to God. Sometimes it points to God's *holiness, moral purity,* and *goodness.* Other times the focus is on *truth* and *revelation.* It is certainly possible John wished to communicate all these ideas here. But is any one of them the primary thought? Given how John uses the concept of "light" in his Gospel, I believe another idea may have been at the forefront of John's intention.

John 1:4 says, "Life was in Him, and that life was the light of men." And in John 8:12 Jesus says, "I am the light of the world. Anyone who follows Me will never walk in the darkness but will have the light of life." In 1 John the statement "God is light" means God has as His very nature and being the source of life. In our God there is light that leads to life. There is not the slightest hint of darkness and death. Martin Luther said, "There is no darkness in him, not even the slightest" (quoted in Akin, *1, 2, 3 John,* 69). There is no "dark side" in this God! Light in this instance equals life (cf. Job 33:28,30). This light leading to life is found in the gospel message about Jesus (1 John 1:5) and proclaimed (1:3,5) by those who have met Him in conversion, which is the new birth (3:9; 5:1,4,18). In the light of God is the fullness of the life of God, and there is no lack of life in Him at all.

This is a non-negotiable tenet in faithful theology and faithful gospel proclamation. This is a message we must be passionate to share with the world. We who have received the light must be a light to the world (cf. Matt 5:14). It must become a central intention of all of our lives to take this light into the darkest of places. As John Falconer said, "I have but one candle of life to burn, and I would rather burn it out in a land filled with darkness than in a land flooded with light" (in Sills, *The Missionary Call,* 181). C. T. Studd would add, "Some want to live within the sound of church or chapel bell; I want to run a rescue shop within a yard of hell" (Hannah, "C T Studd").

The World Must Know What God Says about Sin
1 JOHN 1:6-10

In a real sense, the essence of sin is our attempting to take the place of God. We want to be in charge. We want to establish the ground rules and lay out the playing field. And we want to provide our own definitions of what is right and what is wrong, what sin is and what sin is not. John, on the other hand, is not interested in human opinions on the matter of sin. Divine revelation will set the bar and establish the truth. John seems to be telling us, "Let's hear God's mind on the matter." We will discover that He takes sin very seriously. John rhetorically uses three "If we say" statements to help us see sin as we ought, to see sin as God sees sin. In the process, a healthy theology of lying is addressed.

Do Not Lie to Others (1 John 1:6-7)

Using an inclusive "we" (to indicate anyone, anywhere, at any time who takes this position, as well as John himself), John makes a negative assertion (1:6) and a positive observation (1:7). If we say we have fellowship with God—that God is our intimate friend, known in light and life—yet we walk in darkness—in death and all that accompanies spiritual death and darkness (cf. Eph 2:1-3)—we lie and do not practice or live out the truth. The verb "walk" is in the present tense and speaks of a continuous and consistent pattern of life. In essence, we say to others, "I know God," but our beliefs and behavior contradict our words. By denying that Jesus is God in the flesh and downplaying the seriousness of sin, we lie to others about who we are.

In contrast, verse 7 says that if we live our lives in the realm of light, as God is in the light, we indeed have fellowship (intimate friendship) with one another (1:3-4), and the blood of Jesus his Son keeps on cleansing us from all sin. I love what Martin Luther said about Christ's cleansing blood:

> It is strange that although we preach about the blood and the suffering of Christ every year, yet we see so many sects bursting forth. Oh, the great darkness of the past! But if we cling to the Word that has been made known, we have this treasure, which

is the blood of Christ. If we are beset by sins, no harm is done. The blood of Christ was not shed for the devil or the angels; it was shed for sinners. Accordingly, when I feel sin, why should I despair, and why should I not believe that it has been forgiven? For the blood of Christ washes sins away. The main thing is that we cling simply to the Word. Then there is no trouble. (Luther, *Lectures*, 228)

Do Not Lie to Yourself (1 John 1:8-9)

Those who live in death and darkness do not just lie to others, saying one thing while believing and living another. Eventually they lie to themselves, becoming self-deceived. Their internal spiritual and moral compass goes haywire and their conscience is, as Paul said, "seared" (1 Tim 4:2).

John then introduces his second "If we say" statement. Here we discover what appears to be a claim of sinlessness, a declaration that we are free from the guilt and penalty of sin. This spiritual posture says, "I have no sin and I do not need Jesus as an advocate or atonement." John's judgment on such persons is quick and pointed: they deceive themselves and the truth is not in them. John's message is clear: "You say you have no sin, but God says you do. You say you have no need of a Savior, but God says you do."

John then follows up with the positive and correct theological antidote in verse 9. It is one of the most beloved and memorized verses in the Bible. A free paraphrase of it may help us capture afresh the heart of its marvelous truth: "If we are characterized as those who are continually agreeing with God about our sin, both its nature and its acts, God is both faithful and just (true to Himself) to forgive us our sins and to purify us from all our wickedness." It is as if John were saying, "Look! There are some who cover and conceal their sin. They are liars. There are also confessors who acknowledge and admit their sin. They are forgiven." Proverbs 28:13 reminds us, "The one who conceals his sins will not prosper, but whoever confesses and renounces them will find mercy." The great Baptist preacher Charles Spurgeon got it exactly right:

> The idea of having no sin is a delusion; you are altogether deceived if you say so; the truth is not in you, and you have not seen things in the true light; you must have shut your eyes to

the high requirements of the law, you must be a stranger to your own heart, you must be blind to your own conduct every day, and you must have forgotten to search your thoughts and to weigh your motives, or you would have detected the presence of sin. He who cannot find water in the sea is not more foolish than the man who cannot perceive sin in his members. As the salt flavors every drop of the Atlantic, so does sin affect every atom of our nature. (Spurgeon, "Honest Dealings with God")

It should be noted that the apostle John does not deny our need to be seen as sinless. He simply notes that we cannot find it in ourselves. We need an advocate. We need an atonement. We need another.

Do Not Lie about God (1 John 1:10)

In *The Brothers Karamazov*, Dostoyevsky writes,

The one who lies to himself and believes his own lies comes to a point where he can distinguish no truth either within himself or around him, and thus enters into a state of disrespect towards himself and others. Respecting no one, he loves no one, and to amuse and divert himself in the absence of love, he gives himself up to his passions and his vulgar delights and becomes a complete animal in his vices, and all of it from lying to other people and himself. (*The Brothers Karamazov*, 45)

John says something similar but more simply: lie to others (1:6) and lie to yourself (1:8), and soon you will lie about God. In fact you will actually call God a liar.

John introduces his third "If we say" statement. Again the theological claim he is addressing is that we now live in a state of sinlessness. We claim to be right with God, to believe the truth, and to live without sin. John says with a double punch we are twice wrong. First, we make God a liar because He says we are sinners. Second, His Word is not in those who claim they have no sin problem. Someone *else's* word says we have no sin problem. But *God* says we are sinners and need a Savior. False teachers say we are not sinners and need no Savior. The differing claims are clear aren't they? Which are you going to believe?

The World Must Know What God Says about Jesus
1 JOHN 2:1-2

Modern studies on the historical Jesus can be fascinating. They can also be deceiving and disappointing because they are so far removed in truth and time from the Jesus revealed in the Bible. In a book entitled *The Historical Jesus: Five Views*, it is noted that modernist options include:

> [A]n eschatological prophet, a Galilean holy man, an occultic magician, an innovative rabbi, a trance-inducing psychotherapist, a Jewish sage, a political revolutionary, an Essene conspirator, an itinerant exorcist, an historicized myth, a protoliberation theologian, a peasant artisan, a Torah-observant Pharisee, a Cynic-like philosopher, a self-conscious eschatological agent, a socioeconomic reformer, a paradoxical Messianic claimant and, finally, as one who saw himself as, in some sense, the very embodiment of Yahweh-God. (Beilby and Eddy, *The Historical Jesus*, 53)

I would argue that it is the last one that matches up with Scripture. And this one who is "the very embodiment of Yahweh-God" is both our advocate and our atonement in His work of redemption. Who could ever have imagined or made up anything like this? This Jesus may not be a Jesus we can be comfortable with, but He is the Jesus we need and the whole world needs! In the *Chronicles of Narnia* one of the Penvency children asks of the great Lion-king Aslan, "Is he safe?" The answer: "No! But he is good!" Oh how true that is of the Lion-King of Judah!

Jesus Is Our Advocate (1 John 2:1)

For the first of seven times in this letter John uses the phrase "my little children." It is a term of endearment and fatherly concern. John sees himself as their spiritual father and they as his spiritual children. They stand in striking contrast to the liars of chapter 1. John says, "As a spiritual father, now a spiritual grandfather (cf. Deut 6:1-9), I am writing to you these things, the things of 1:5-10, so that you may not sin." John has made it clear that in this life we cannot be sinless (but note again the future promise of 3:2!), but he does believe we can sin less because we are now in intimate fellowship with the Father and His Son, Jesus Christ (1:3).

We will still sin until we are glorified. What do we do when we sin? Well, in 1:9 he told us to confess our sins. Now in 2:1 he tells us to flee to our Savior who is our "advocate with the Father—Jesus Christ the Righteous One." The word "advocate" is *parakletos* in Greek, or paraclete. The word occurs five times in the New Testament (John 14:16,26; 15:25; 16:7; 1 John 2:1). Four times it refers to the Holy Spirit. Only here is it a reference to the Lord Jesus who is able to be our advocate because He is "the Righteous One." Isaiah 53:11 may be echoed here. There our Lord is called Yahweh's "righteous Servant." This advocate is sinless, undefiled, and spotless in His nature and in all of His actions. There is no one else like Him.

The word "advocate" means helper, one who is called to come alongside in a time of need. This helper helps us when we sin. He is the cleanser of sin (1:7), the forgiver of sin (1:9), and the helper when we do sin. Isn't the gospel amazing? We have a helper in our heart (the Holy Spirit) and a helper in heaven (Jesus Christ the Righteous One). Or as Paul says, we have an intercessor in our hearts (Rom 8:26-27) and an intercessor in heaven (Rom 8:35). As a result, no sin can "separate us from the love of God that is in Christ Jesus our Lord!" (Rom 8:39).

Jesus Is Our Atonement (1 John 2:2)

John now informs us why Jesus can be our advocate. It is because He made a "propitiation," an atonement for our sins. The word "propitiation" is a very important word in the New Testament. It is the Greek word *hilasmos*. The word and its variants occur in the context of the work of Christ in four crucial texts: Rom 3:25; Heb 2:17; 1 John 2:2; 4:10. The word carries the idea of satisfaction. Jesus Christ, by His bloody sacrifice on the cross, satisfied God's holiness and turned away His righteous wrath from sinners. The wrath that should have been poured out on sinners was poured out on Jesus. The judgment that should have been experienced by sinners was experienced by Jesus. The hell that should have been experienced by sinners was experienced by Jesus.

All this was done to accomplish God's purpose. Second Corinthians 5:19 reveals that through this propitiation, "in Christ, God was reconciling the world to Himself." Therefore feminist theologian Delores Williams is wrong when she says, "There is nothing divine in the blood of the cross" (Williams, *Sisters in the Wilderness*, 61). And Episcopal bishop John Spong misses it when he says, "Neither do I want a God who would kill his own son" (quoted in Ash, "Bishop Will Retire But He Won't Stop"). Steve Chalke is also in error when he says the orthodox understanding of the cross is a form of cosmic child abuse, "a vengeful

father, punishing his son for an offence he has not even committed
. . . [a] twisted version of events morally dubious and a huge barrier
to faith" (Chalke and Mann, *The Lost Message of Jesus*, 182–83). No, the
work of atonement accomplished by Christ on the cross is where God's
holiness and God's love meet, where God's judgment and God's mercy
kiss. Yes, it pleased the Father to crush His Son and put Him to grief
(Isa 53:10), and it pleased the Father to highly exalt Him and bestow on
Him "the name that is above every name" (Phil 2:9).

And it is important to note that there is a universal component to
this atoning work: it is "for [the sins] of the whole world." No one is
beyond its reach. No one. A universal provision has been made so that
as the redeemed so awesomely sing in Revelation 5:9, "You are worthy
to take the scroll and to open its seals, because You were slaughtered,
and You redeemed people for God by Your blood from every tribe and
language and people and nation."

Conclusion

The wonderful Church Father Augustine (AD 354–430) well said,

> For we could not be redeemed, even through the one
> Mediator between God and men, the man Christ Jesus, if He
> were not also God. Now when Adam was created, he, being a
> righteous man, had no need of a mediator. But when sin had
> placed a wide gulf between God and the human race, it was
> expedient that a Mediator, who alone of the human race was
> born, lived, and died without sin, should reconcile us to God,
> and procure even for our bodies a resurrection to eternal life.
> (*Enchiridion*, ch. 108)

Malcolm Muggeridge (1903–1990) would add,

> I have conscientiously looked far and wide, inside and outside
> my own head and heart, and I have found nothing other
> than this man and his words which offers any answer to the
> dilemmas of this tragic, troubled time. If his light has gone
> out, then, as far as I am concerned, there is no light. (*Seeing
> through the Eye*, 106)

Thankfully, the light has not gone out. It has come in the person of Jesus
Christ. So, let us flee to it. Then, let us take it to the world, a world for
which He and He alone is the propitiation, the perfect atoning sacrifice.

Reflect and Discuss

1. How has our culture come to take sin lightly? How do we do this in our own lives?
2. Why is it important to realize that the gospel message has not changed?
3. Light is a common theme in Scripture. How does the image of light help you understand who God is?
4. How does the truth that Jesus is "the light of the world" fuel missions around the world?
5. Why is it important to get our idea of sin from what God says rather than from our culture?
6. What is the relationship between belief and action according to John? What do your actions say about your relationship with Christ?
7. Why should Christians be marked by continual confession of sin?
8. What are some options about Jesus' identity that you have heard? How do they match up with Scripture?
9. Because all men are sinners, what does John say about Jesus that gives us hope? How does Jesus fulfill the roles of advocate and atoning sacrifice?
10. How does Christ's coming mandate global missions?

Know and Obey to Be Happy in Jesus

1 JOHN 2:3-11

Main Idea: True followers of Jesus will have assurance in their salvation because they know, love, and obey Him.

I. **Obey Christ's Commands and Enjoy the Assurance of Salvation (2:3-6).**
   A. You will know that you know Him (2:3-4).
   B. You will know His love perfectly (2:5).
   C. You will know you are abiding in Christ (2:6).
II. **Love One Another and Walk in the Light of Salvation (2:7-11).**
   A. God's love has been with us since conversion (2:7).
   B. God's love is seen most truly in Jesus and His followers (2:8).
   C. God's love exposes the darkness of hatred (2:9-11).

Is it possible to know God and to live like the Devil? Is it possible to truly know God and have no life change? Adrian Rogers answered these questions this way: "Study the Bible to know about God. Obey the Bible to really know God" (*Adrianisms*, 33). The apostle John would agree. He explained in 1 John that it is one thing to say you know God, but it is another to really know Him. To help us be "sure that we have come to know Him" (2:3), John provides a threefold test that he returns to again and again in this letter. We can put them in the form of three questions. First, do I believe the right things about Jesus? We may call this the *theological* test. Second, do I obey the commands of God? This is the *moral* test. Third, do I love others? This is the *ethical* test. John addressed the theological test in 1:5–2:2. Now he will address the moral test in 2:3-6 and the ethical test in 2:7-11. His goal is that you and I would live in the assurance of our salvation and thereby be happy in Jesus all the days of our lives.

Obey Christ's Commands and Enjoy the Assurance of Salvation

1 JOHN 2:3-6

Chuck Colson (1931–2012) of Watergate and Prison Fellowship fame wrote a masterpiece entitled *Loving God*. In it he said the essence of the Christian life is obedience:

> "But how do we love the Lord?" we ask. Jesus answered this in a discussion with His disciples: "If you love me, you will obey what I command" (John 14:15). Or, as the apostle John wrote later, "This is the love of God, that we keep his commandments" (1 John 5:3). (*Loving God*, 40)

Dietrich Bonheoffer similarly states, "Only he who believes is obedient; only he who is obedient believes" (quoted in Colson, *Loving God*, 19). Both to love Him and to know Him is to obey Him. Knowing God and loving God are intimately wed ideas in 1 John (he will use the words more than 40 times each in this five-chapter letter), and both of them lead to obedience. To know God is to love God and to love God is to obey God. This obedience, John teaches us, reveals the genuineness of our faith (2:3), the authenticity of our confession (v. 4), the maturing of our love (v. 5), and our growth in Christlikeness (v. 6). For John—and it should be the same for us—there is a massive difference between merely saying and actually doing, between merely saying and truly knowing (1:6,8,10; 2:4,6,9). Matt Carter applies this truth in this way:

> When I am participating in an interview with someone we're thinking about adding to our [church] staff . . . I let others ask the detailed questions. I ask the candidate only one question. I ask him or her, "When was the last time the thought of the gospel made you weep?" If the person we're interviewing can't answer the question, I simply won't hire him or her. Why? Because I've realized there is a direct connection between a person's love for Jesus and that person's obedience to Him. (McCoy and Carter, *The Real Win*, 135)

What would your answer be? It is a really good question.

You Will Know That You Know Him (1 John 2:3-4)

John saw the importance of the gospel's connection to obedience. He knew it was an important avenue for assurance of salvation. If you want to know day by day that you know Him, that you are saved, it is simple: look to His perfect advocacy and atoning work on your behalf (vv. 1-2) and keep His commands. The word "keeping" conveys the idea of guarding. We should guard God's commands as a precious treasure. And as we do, the treasure of our assurance of salvation is strengthened with it. Obedience is an important avenue of assurance. Because I know Him in all of His beauty, glory, and majesty, I delight in obeying Him. To obey Christ is not a burden. It is a blessing. It is my natural response to what He has done for me.

However, if we claim to know Him but do not guard His commands as precious (v. 4), we are liars (what we say) and the truth is not in us (who we are). We are spiritual deceivers, fakes. We claim to have something we really don't: a true and genuine relationship with God.

The new birth (cf. John 3) that results from fleeing to Jesus as our advocate and our atonement will place a new knowledge in our minds and a new desire and passion in our hearts to obey Him. That desire to obey and our decision to obey give us a certainty that we know Him.

You Will Know His Love Perfectly (1 John 2:5)

Keeping the commands of God is not a condition of knowing God, but it is a clear sign and indication that we do know God. It is a life of true worship that delights in the commands of God for no other reason than it delights in the God who gives those commands. John says, "But whoever keeps [as a habit and pattern of life] His word [His commands], truly in him the love of God is perfected." This verse is set in contrast to verse 4, and it advances the argument John is making. It also ties together the vital relationship of knowing God, loving God, and obeying God. This is a powerful triad, to say the least.

The phrase "love of God" is ambiguous and open to various understandings. It could mean God's love for us, our love for God, God's kind of love, or simply the love of God in a general sense. I believe the context here indicates it is our love for God that is in view. As we consistently obey God, carefully guarding His Word, our love for God grows and is brought to maturity and completion. It reaches a marked-out-in-advance goal and is brought to perfection (cf. 4:12,17,18). In keeping

and obeying His Word, my love for Jesus grows, matures, and is brought
to its intended goal. And here is the beauty of the whole thing: the more
I know Him the more I love Him, and the more I love Him the more I
know Him. The same thing happens in a godly marriage. It should be
that the more a husband and wife grow to know one another, the more
they love one another. And the more love they share with each other,
the more they will desire to know each other.

There is a tradition that on one occasion the apostle John, near
the end of his life, was brought to the church on a pallet. All he said to
the believing community was, "Love one another." When he was asked
why that was all he had to say, he responded, "Because it is enough."
The perfecting of our love life is an additional avenue "that we are in
Him"—that we belong to Jesus and that Jesus belongs to us.

You Will Know You Are Abiding in Christ (1 John 2:6)

When God saved us He did not save us simply to take us to heaven. He
saved us that we might be conformed to His perfect image—that we
might become like Jesus (Rom 8:29; 1 John 3:2). He saved us that we
might "walk just as He walked."

Verse 6 is the second "the one who says" statement in this section (cf.
vv. 4,9). Here John speaks of our remaining, or abiding, in Him. Jesus
said a lot about this in John 15. So will John. He will use this word 23
times in this epistle (Gk *meno*, translated "remain" in HCSB). Like obeying Jesus and loving Jesus, abiding in Christ is the natural outgrowth of
knowing Him. The idea is one of continuing in Jesus.

John says we have both a statement to prove and a Savior to imitate.
And the word "should" conveys a moral obligation for our walk to match
our talk. To truly abide in Christ means I will live (walk) like Christ. This
theme is not unique to 1 John but is repeated several times in the New
Testament.

> *Remain in Me, and I in you. Just as a branch is unable to produce
> fruit by itself unless it remains on the vine, so neither can you unless
> you remain in Me. I am the vine; you are the branches. The one who
> remains in Me and I in him produces much fruit, because you can do
> nothing without Me.* (John 15:4-5)

> *Imitate me, as I also imitate Christ.* (1 Cor 11:1)

> *Therefore, be imitators of God, as dearly loved children.* (Eph 5:1)

*For you were called to this, because Christ also suffered for you, leaving
you an example, so that you should follow in His steps.* (1 Pet 2:21)

Like Father, like Son. Like Savior, like saint. Christ's life becomes my
life, my example, my goal, and my pattern. And we must note that it
is abiding in Him that enables me to live like Him. I don't do it in my
strength. I do it in His! I don't have to be like Him to be assured, I want
to be like Him and am assured. John Stott says, "We cannot claim to
abide in Him unless we are like Him" (Stott, *The Letters of John*, 97). But
as we abide in Him we will be like Him because we will know Him.

Love One Another and Walk in the Light of Salvation
1 JOHN 2:7-11

John is good at simplifying the Christian life. Basically he says to know
Jesus, obey God, and love others. Briefly introduced in verse 5, John will
now give more intense attention to the theme of our love life. In verse
5 it was our love for God that concerned the apostle. Now in verses 7-11
he must address urgently our love for others.

John begins with an affirmation of his love for those to whom he is
writing. He calls them "dear friends" or "beloved." It is the Greek word
agapetoi, and John will use it six times in this letter (2:7; 3:2,21; 4:1,7,11).
It is a term of endearment, of heart-felt love and concern. It usually
serves John well as he begins a new thought. In this instance, though,
it allows him to continue and expand on the idea of God's commands.
Here he will narrow his focus to one specific command: the command
to love. Interestingly, though the idea of love is clearly the theme of this
section, the word itself only appears in verse 10.

This section raises the question: Does John believe a right love for
God (v. 5) is absolutely essential for a right love toward our brothers
(v. 10)? I believe the answer is a resounding Yes! Indeed the two are
inseparable.

God's Love Has Been with Us Since Conversion (1 John 2:7)

I believe the Gospel of John was written before the letters of John and
that the letters of John assume a knowledge of the Gospel of John. Here
it is John 13:34-35 that John assumes his audience knows. In that passage
Jesus said, "I give you a new command: Love one another. Just as I have
loved you, you must also love one another. By this all people will know

that you are My disciples, if you have love for one another." This being
the case, John can say the command to love one another is not new;
rather, it is old. It is something you have had from the beginning, the
beginning of your Christian experience as a follower of Jesus. Further,
you know of this command's ancient root in Leviticus 19:18, what Jesus
called the second great command. There Moses wrote, "Do not take
revenge or bear a grudge against members of your community, but love
your neighbor as yourself, I am Yahweh." Speaking about 1 John 2:7,
John Piper says,

> This [verse] is a very remarkable rebuke to typical gospel
> preaching and witnessing today. For John, the commandment
> of love belongs to what people should hear from the
> beginning! It is not an optional stage two in Christian growth.
> . . . The gospel contains not only the commandment to trust
> Jesus, but also the commandment, in the power of that trust,
> to be changed into a loving person. ("The One Who Lives In
> Light")

God's Love Is Seen Most Truly in Jesus and His Followers (1 John 2:8)

Some cynics might argue that the apostle John leaves himself open
to the charge of senility in verse 8. After all, in verse 7 he says, "I am
not writing you a new command but an old command." Now in verse
8 he says, "Yet I am writing you a new command." Well, which is it? The
answer is, "It is both." I think the opening phrase as translated by the
ESV is helpful when it says, "At the same time." This old, old command
goes all the way back to Moses, but it took on a new character with the
coming of Jesus. This is his point. And the newness is threefold. First,
it is new and true in Jesus. Second, it is true and new in us, those who
"walk just as He walked" (v. 6). Third, it is true and new in us because
"the darkness is passing away and the true light is already shining" (cf.
John 1:5,9).

In Christ the command to love one another is strengthened, deep-
ened, expanded, and given a depth of meaning and understanding
never seen before His coming in the incarnation. And now that same
kind of supernatural love is being seen and experienced in those who
love Him and abide in Him. But there's more! Perfect love as revealed
in the life, death, and resurrection of Jesus Christ has dealt a death blow

to darkness. Darkness is on the run and it cannot outrun the light. In fact the darkness is already departing and the true light already shines! The light of the world (John 8:12) has come. The King of light and love is already reigning, and the fullness and consummation of that reign is just around the corner. How we love one another gives evidence of all of this. Love is not new. It is as old as God (1 John 4:8) and rooted in the law. Yet it is new to us in conversion and new in its depth in Jesus. It is new in experience, emphasis, expression, and endurance. It is old as the sun and new as the dawn.

God's Love Exposes the Darkness of Hatred (1 John 2:9-11)

John utilizes his third "the one who says" statement, and he does so to draw the strongest possible contrast between those who are in the light and those who are in the darkness, between those who love and those who hate, between those who are the children of God and those who are the children of the Devil (3:10). Verse 9 essentially says, "If you say you are in the light experiencing the life of God, yet you continually hate your brother, only one conclusion can be drawn: You are still in darkness, the realm of spiritual death and moral corruption, evil and wickedness. You still belong to the Devil." Verse 10 provides the contrast: "If you are consistently loving your brother, you continually abide in light and give evidence that you have the life of God in you." Further, there is no cause for stumbling (Gk, *scandalon*) or offense for the one who abides in the realm of light. He truly is walking as Jesus walked (v. 6). The world of light and love always go together.

Verse 11 returns to those who are in darkness: If you continually hate your brother, four things are true for you: First, you are in the darkness (spiritual death). Second, you walk (live) in darkness. Third, you do not know where you are going. And fourth, you are blind. In the darkness of spiritual death there is the absence of love and the absence of God in our lives. And tragically, we don't even see it, having lived so long in the darkness. We are like blind men in a dark room who have no idea where they are or where they are going. It is a true tragedy.

Conclusion

There is an old hymn titled "Trust and Obey" with text by John H. Sammis. The first verse and refrain read,

When we walk with the Lord
in the light of His Word,
what a glory He sheds on our way!
While we do His good will,
He abides with us still,
and with all who will trust and obey.

Trust and obey,
for there's no other way
to be happy in Jesus,
but to trust and obey.

I believe the apostle John would have liked this song. I believe he would have agreed with its message. You see, to trust Him, you must first know Him—know Him as the One who has been from the beginning; know Him as the One who is the Word of life and the eternal life; know Him as the Son of the Father in whom there in no darkness at all; know Him as the cleanser and forgiver of sins; know Him as your advocate and atonement. To know Him is to trust Him, and to trust Him is to obey Him. And when you do, you will experience a happiness in Jesus that will indeed be a glory that He will shed on your way.

Reflect and Discuss

1. How would you explain to your friends that obedience, as the Bible describes it, is not an oppressive idea?
2. What is the relationship between obedience and assurance for the Christian? What assurances come with a life of obedience?
3. Why does truly knowing God lead to obedience to His commands?
4. How can God be loving if He commands obedience from His people?
5. What does it mean to abide or remain in Christ? What other passages of Scripture would you use to shed light on this idea?
6. Is it possible to rightly love others without a true love for God? How does John shed light on this question?
7. How is John's command to love one another both old and new? How does this give weight to John's argument?
8. What are some examples of love that you see throughout the Scriptures? How is Jesus the perfect example of love for one another?

9. Why is hatred for a brother contrary to love for God? What does such hatred expose about our hearts?
10. How can you live out love for others in such a way that reveals your knowledge of and love for God?

The Love God Hates

1 JOHN 2:12-17

Main Idea: Those who truly love and follow Christ must not fall in love with the things of this world, but rather with the Father who gives them everything they need.

I. **Know What You Are in Christ and Cannot Lose (2:12-14).**
   A. You are forgiven (2:12).
   B. You know the Father (2:13-14).
   C. You are victors in the faith (2:13-14).
II. **Know What the World Offers but Cannot Give (2:15-17).**
   A. The world cannot give you what you need (2:15).
   B. The world cannot give you what it promises (2:16).
   C. The world cannot give you what will last (2:17).

I was blessed to grow up in a home with a godly mother who taught me to love Jesus and believe the Bible. When I was young, I remember asking my mom, "Does God hate the Devil?" She answered me in the way a little boy probably needed answering: "Honey, God doesn't hate anybody. He loves everyone and everything and so should we." I am sure that probably is what I needed to hear at the time. However, I have since learned that my mother's well-intended answer was not altogether correct. The fact is, the Bible teaches there are some things God hates, and so should we.

The boastful cannot stand in Your presence; You hate all evildoers. You destroy those who tell lies; the Lord abhors a man of bloodshed and treachery. (Ps 5:5-6)

You who love the Lord, hate evil! He protects the lives of His godly ones; He rescues them from the power of the wicked. (Ps 97:10)

I gain understanding from Your precepts; therefore I hate every false way. (Ps 119:104)

I hate those who are double-minded, but I love Your instruction. (Ps 119:113)

I hate and abhor falsehood, but I love Your instruction. (Ps 119:163)

The Lord hates six things; in fact, seven are detestable to Him: arrogant eyes, a lying tongue, hands that shed innocent blood, a heart that plots wicked schemes, feet eager to run to evil, a lying witness who gives false testimony, and one who stirs up trouble among brothers. (Prov 6:16-19)

You have loved righteousness and hated lawlessness; this is why God, Your God, has anointed You with the oil of joy rather than Your companions. (Heb 1:9)

Yet you do have this: You hate the practices of the Nicolaitans, which I also hate. (Rev 2:6)

Our text could rightly be added to this list. Interestingly, and surprisingly, that which God hates, which He stands in strong opposition to, is a particular kind of love, namely love for the world (1 John 2:15). James 4:4 teaches us to not even make friends with the world because to do so is to become "an enemy of God." Here John teaches us not to love the world, for if we do, "love for the Father is not in [us]" (v. 15).

At first glance, verses 12-14 and 15-17 do not seem to go together. However, on closer inspection we see that they complement each other beautifully. Verses 12-14 provide the encouragement necessary to heed the exhortation of verses 15-17. We belong to God. We know Him as Father. We are part of His family. He is our Father and heaven is our home. It is hardly conceivable that, knowing this, we would give our affections to the things of this life, this world. If we know God as Father, we will not set our hearts on the fleeting and transitory things of a system and worldview perspective that stands in defiant opposition to Him.

Know What You Are in Christ and Cannot Lose
1 JOHN 2:12-14

C. S. Lewis said it well: "Fallen man is not simply an imperfect creature who needs improvement: he is a rebel who must lay down his arms" (*Mere Christianity*, 56). And, as we surrender, God not only takes us into His kingdom, but He also brings us into His family. We become His children (vv. 12-13), and He becomes our Father (v. 13). We become strong in Him, His Word takes up residence in us, and we gain victory over Satan, who is "the evil one" (v. 14; cf. 4:4).

Verses 12-14 are beautifully structured, rhythmic and poetic. Six times John says, "I am writing" (vv. 12-13) or "I have written" (vv. 13-14). Three different terms are used to identify his audience: "children," "fathers," and "young men," and each group is addressed twice for emphasis. Now, why does John address his readers in this fashion? Perhaps he has in mind all believers—new believers, older believers, and maturing believers. This makes sense, since there is little doubt that he is addressing us in terms of spiritual maturity and not chronological age. I do like the way John Piper answers the question:

> I think the three groups of "children," "fathers," and "young men" originated something like this. In these verses John wants to reach out to the church with affection and encouragement. So he begins by calling them children, just like he does five other times (2:1,18; 3:18; 4:4; 5:21).
>
> Then he pauses and thinks: "I certainly don't want to give offense to the leaders in the church—the venerable old men or the virile young men—with this affectionate term 'children.' Perhaps I should address these two groups: the venerable fathers have knowledge, and the virile young men have conquered." But don't skip over these verses if you don't happen to be in one of those groups. What is true for them is true for all believers. ("The Strong Need Strength")

You Are Forgiven (1 John 2:12)

John begins with one of the most simple and basic truths of Christianity: we have been forgiven for all of our sins because of "Jesus' name." This speaks to both the person and the work of Christ, especially His perfect atoning work (v. 2). Matthew 1:21 reminds us that the angel said to Joseph, "She [Mary] will give birth to a son, and you are to name Him Jesus, because He will save His people from their sins." Jesus cleanses us from all sin (1 John 1:7) and unrighteousness (1:9). He is faithful to forgive all the sins of those who trust in Him. Having run to Jesus as our advocate and atonement (2:1-2), we have been welcomed by God as His children. What a wonderful truth it is that "the name of Yahweh is a strong tower; the righteous run to it and are protected" (Prov 18:10).

You Know the Father (1 John 2:13-14)

When we receive Jesus as our Savior we also get God as our Father (cf. v. 23). John says to the fathers in the faith, "you have come to know the One who is from the beginning" (v. 13). The reference to the "One" may be to the Father or even to Christ, or possibly both. Of course both are true. We now know in an abiding, permanent relationship the One who has existed from all creation and the One whom we see in the Gospels. Echoes of John 1:1 and 1 John 1:1 ring out in our spiritual ears. He repeats this wonderful truth in verse 14. He doesn't want us to forget it. There is a deep and abiding knowledge that has grown throughout our Christian experience. The longer we have lived, the deeper and better we know Him.

John then says to the children in verse 14, "You have come to know the Father." The beauty of this statement is in its simplicity. The One who is God is now our Father. And He is a good Father, a great Father, a perfect Father. No longer is He our enemy, but through forgiveness of sins and His gracious adoption, we have come to know Him as Father. These promises of forgiveness of sin and knowledge of God reflect the New Covenant promises of Jeremiah 31:31-34. In verse 34 we read:

> "No longer will one teach his neighbor or his brother, saying, 'Know the Lord,' for they will all know Me, from the least to the greatest of them"—this is the Lord's declaration. "For I will forgive their wrongdoing and never again remember their sin."

You Are Victors in the Faith (1 John 2:13-14)

Warriors in the faith are now addressed by the term "young men." These are believers who are maturing in the faith, young champions for Christ who are actively engaged in spiritual warfare against Satan, identified as the "evil one" in verses 13 and 14. Three distinctive observations can be made about the young men who are at war with the Devil: they are strong, the Word of God abides in them, and they have overcome the evil one. There is no doubt in my mind that our strength and our ability to defeat the evil one has a twofold source. One is the work of Christ (cf. 3:8) and the other is the Word of God abiding in us. Satan will accuse us on the one hand and tempt us on the other. The work of Christ answers his first tactic, and the Word of God addresses the second. When Satan accuses me of sin, I trust the work of Christ. My debt has been paid, and while Satan can hurl accusations all day long, he has nothing with which he can condemn me (Rom 8:1). Also, when Satan tempts me to sin, I turn to the Word of God. I am again helped by the way John Piper summarizes how the work of Christ and the Word of God empower us to gain victory and overcome the evil one (v. 14).

1. Jesus Christ, the righteous (v. 1), died in our place.
2. The wrath of God is propitiated; its removal is sealed.
3. Christ is raised from the dead and intercedes as our advocate in heaven on the basis of that propitiation.
4. The Word of God—the gospel—comes to us and by grace we receive it and it abides in us.
5. In this way, we abide in Christ so that *he becomes our personal propitiation and advocate*, that is, we experience what Christ obtained for us.
6. Satan accuses us of damning sin and tries to destroy us with guilt.
7. We—like the young men of 1 John 2:14—overcome the evil one because the word of God abides in us and we are strong (Piper, "The Word of God Abides in You").

Know What the World Offers but Cannot Give
1 JOHN 2:15-17

Having provided a word of encouragement in verses 12-14, John now gives a word of exhortation and warning concerning something he identifies six times as "the world." Here he is not using the word "world" (Gk *cosmos*) to speak of God's good creation (Acts 17:24) or even the world of people for whom Christ died (1 John 2:2; John 3:16). No, instead he is referring here to a worldview perspective (cf. John 16:11) that is led by "the evil one" whom we have overcome and that is characterized by the desires of the flesh, the desires of the eyes, and pride in possessions (1 John 2:16). To love the world is to be devoid of love for the Father (v. 15) and to give ourselves to things that are temporary and transient, things that have no lasting or eternal value.

Worldliness or "being of the world" is often misunderstood. Often it is identified with cultural issues that are of a particular concern to us. John is not telling us to reject any and all aspects of culture, much of which reflects the glory, goodness, and gifts of God. What he is telling us is we are not to love and idolize thoughts, values, and behaviors that are contrary to God's Word (v. 14) and His will (v. 17). Things that appeal to our sinful flesh (e.g., drug abuse, drunkenness, gluttony, abundance of possessions, sexual perversions, etc.) and are fleeting and passing are not to be the things that we live for. My friend Mark Driscoll put it like this:

> John describes worldliness as the cravings of our sinful flesh (gluttony, sexual perversion, drunkenness, etc.), lust of our eyes (sexual lust, coveting, etc.), and arrogant pride that causes us to boast in ourselves without ever thanking God. In our age filled with advertising, rock stars, supermodels and celebrities, it is not an overstatement to say that if worldliness means living only to please our flesh and pursue what our eyes lust after—so that we can arrogantly boast about our conquests and accomplishments—then worldliness is a synonym for America. Therefore, John reminds us that the world is going to burn up in the end; but if we belong to God we will live forever with Him, and so we must remain ever vigilant to love God and not the world. (*1, 2 & 3 John: Walking in the Light*)

John highlights three things the world promises but cannot deliver. His words are strong medicine that can bring healing to our souls.

The World Cannot Give You What You Need (1 John 2:15)

The longing of the human heart is to be loved and to love. The objects of our affections need to be rightly ordered if we are truly to find ultimate and lasting satisfaction. John, therefore, commands us, "Do not love the world or the things that belong to the world." Why? To love the world is to *not* love Father God, which is what you really need. It is what you were created for. John says, "Choose your lover, but choose carefully; choose wisely. Choose God the Father, not the worldly enticements of the father of lies" (John 8:44). We must recognize that turning even good things into "god" things becomes a bad thing. It is to give your love to a lesser lover—one who can never satisfy, who can never give you what you truly need.

The World Cannot Give You What It Promises (1 John 2:16)

This is one of the most important verses in the Bible. It identifies in vivid terms the weapons the world uses to seduce men and women into joining its side. Amazingly, each of these weapons resides in us! The enemy really is within! These same three weapons slew Adam and Eve in the Garden. Genesis 3:6 says, "Then the woman saw that the tree was good for food [lust of the flesh] and delightful to look at [lust of the eyes], and that it was desirable for obtaining wisdom [the pride of life]." These same three weapons were conquered by Christ, the second Adam, in His temptation in the wilderness. Luke 4:1-13 explains that the Devil beckoned Him to "tell this stone to become bread" (Luke 4:3), which is the lust of the flesh. Then he "showed Him all the kingdoms of the world" (Luke 4:5), tempting Jesus with the lust of the eyes. Finally, from the pinnacle of the temple, the Devil challenged him, "If You are the Son of God, throw Yourself down from here. For it is written: He will give His angels orders concerning you, to protect you, and they will support you with their hands, so that you will not strike your foot against a stone" (Luke 4:9-10). But even the pride of life could not lead the Savior into sin.

Seeing how prevalent these temptations are, a close and careful inspection of each weapon will be helpful in our pursuit of spiritual victory. Though they are old, they are still effective if we do not recognize and resist them through the power of the Spirit and the Word of God.

The desires of the flesh appeal to our appetites. "Desires" means cravings, lust, or passion. The word is neutral. The object determines whether such desires are good or bad. John tells us that worldly desires are of the flesh. "Flesh" (Gk *sarx*) may sometimes refer to the whole person, but here it denotes the tendency and bent of humans to fulfill natural desires in a way that is contrary to God's will. For example, sexual appetite gives way to immorality, and physical appetite gives way to gluttony. We give in to the flesh because we are sinful. It is important to realize that we are not sinful because we sin. Instead, we sin because we are sinful. The lust of the flesh is powerful because we are sinful at our core. To us, sin is fun, enticing, and attractive. We are drawn to it like a fly to flypaper, like a fish to a baited hook.

The desire of the eyes appeals to our affections. Our eyes, like our natural desire, are not evil. Proverbs 20:12 says, "The hearing ear and the seeing eye—the Lord made them both." However, the eyes are windows to the mind (soul) by which sinful desires enter in. This is why Jesus said in Matthew 5:27-29,

You have heard that it was said, Do not commit adultery. But I tell you, everyone who looks at a woman to lust for her has already

committed adultery with her in his heart. If your right eye causes you to sin, gouge it out and throw it away. For it is better that you lose one of the parts of your body than for your whole body to be thrown into hell.

Men, being creatures of sight, must especially be on guard here. Remember, it was David's eyes that led him to lie, commit adultery, and murder (2 Sam 11).

Pride in possessions appeals to our ambitions. Pride is vainglory, boasting, or arrogance. It refers to the braggart who exaggerates what he has in order to impress others. It is the "I, me, my" person. "Pride of possessions" or "pride of life" speaks of the person who glorifies himself rather than God. He or she makes an idol of their stuff, their career, their achievements, and their social standing. They suffer from "affluenza!" Pride, power, possessions, prestige, and position are what life is all about. This person fails to see that the Lord Jesus, the King of glory, turned the value system of this world on its head. A. W. Tozer draws our attention to the blinding deception of the "pride in possessions":

> There is within the human heart a tough, fibrous root of fallen life whose nature is to possess, always to possess. It covets "things" with a deep and fierce passion. The pronouns "my" and "mine" look innocent enough in print, but their constant and universal use is significant. They express the real nature of the old Adamic man better than a thousand volumes of theology could do. They are verbal symptoms of our deep disease. The roots of our hearts have grown down into things, and we dare not pull up one rootlet lest we die. Things have become necessary to us, a development never originally intended. God's gifts now take the place of God, and the whole course of nature is upset by the monstrous substitution. (*The Pursuit of God*, 22)

Jesus sets for us a beautiful counter example. Concerning pride in birth and rank, He was a carpenter's son (Matt 13:55), a poor family's child (Luke 2:24; see Lev 12:8). Concerning pride in possessions, He said, "The Son of Man has no place to lay His head" (Matt 8:20). Concerning pride in pedigree, it was said of Him, "Can anything good come out of Nazareth?" (John 1:46). Concerning pride in people, it was said of Him, "[He is] a friend of tax collectors and sinners" (Matt 11:19). Concerning pride in intellect, He said, "As the Father taught

Me, I say these things" (John 8:28). Concerning pride in self-will, He said, "If You are willing, take this cup away from Me—nevertheless, not My will, but Yours, be done" (Luke 22:42).

The example of Jesus is instructive. James 4:6 says, "But [God] gives greater grace. Therefore He says: God resists the proud, but gives grace to the humble." And 1 Peter 5:6 says, "Humble yourselves, therefore, under the mighty hand of God, so that He may exalt you at the proper time." God's newly created beings rightly relate to Him not with a heart of pride, but in a posture of humility, just as Jesus, who was Himself the Creator, demonstrated His entire life.

The World Cannot Give You What Will Last (1 John 2:17)

This verse brings to a conclusion John's argument as he contrasts the two loves, two lives, two approaches to life. Why side with the world? Why give your life to an empty imitation, a worthless fake, a temporary illusion? The world, this evil and deceptive system of Satan, is continually passing away and its desires with it. The darkness was on the run in 2:8. The world is on the run in 2:17. Light and that which will last forever has shown up in Jesus Christ. What remains? What lasts? What endures? The answer is, the one doing (continually) the will of God. This one abides (continually) forever.

Jesus said many things about the will of God, especially in John's Gospel.

> *My food is to do the will of Him who sent Me and to finish His work.*
> (John 4:34)

> *I can do nothing on My own. I judge only as I hear, and My judgment is righteous, because I do not seek My own will, but the will of Him who sent Me.* (John 5:30)

> *For I have come down from heaven, not to do My will, but the will of Him who sent Me.* (John 6:38)

Jesus' work is lasting and effectual because it was the will of the Father for Him to do that work. For our work to abide like Christ's, our hearts must not be attached to the things of this world, but to the will of the Father.

In the book *Embracing Obscurity*, a beautiful contrast is drawn between the things of the world and the things of the Father (Anonymous,

Embracing Obscurity, 87). In the chart below, I have listed differences, making only a few slight adjustments and additions to those in the book. The differences between the two could not be more striking.

Things of the World	Things of the Father
• The focus is on me.	• The focus is on God.
• Make as much money as possible.	• Give as much money away as possible, and spend even yourself on others.
• Live comfortably.	• Life is not about comfort, but about doing hard things now so that we can reap rewards in the life to come.
• Make a name for yourself.	• Make His name great.
• Do whatever makes you happiest.	• Do whatever makes God happiest.
• Teach your children to love themselves and seek self-fulfillment.	• Teach your children to love and obey God. ("Behaving" is often, but not always, a blessed by-product.)
• Look like a model in a magazine and turn your physical appearance into an idol.	• Treat your body as the temple of the Holy Spirit, and cultivate an inner beauty.
• Offer "acts of service" when you feel like it (on your terms).	• Be a servant, even when it is uncomfortable or inconvenient.
• Stay married as long as your spouse meets your needs.	• Serve your spouse (the way Christ modeled servanthood), and choose to love him or her for life.
• Come across as powerful, influential, and/or interesting.	• Give preference to others in words and actions.
• Use (worldly) wisdom to accrue wealth.	• Value true wisdom (which is the fear of God) over all the treasures on earth.
• Stay up to date with the fashions.	• Be content just to have clothes.
• The things of the world are passing away.	• The things of the Father will abide forever.
• I do the will of the world.	• I do the will of the Father.

Conclusion

One of the saddest stories in the Bible concerns a man by the name of Demas. He is not very well known, but his life serves as an important and tragic lesson for those of us who love the Father who sent His Son. We first hear of him in Colossians 4:14 where he is working hard for the gospel alongside Luke. He is listed along with nearly ten others for their faithful service to Christ (Col 4:7-18). We do not hear of him again until 2 Timothy 4:10, toward the end of Paul's last letter, as Paul anticipates his own execution and martyrdom for Christ. There we simply read, "Demas has deserted me, because he loved this present world." The NLT says, "he loves the things of this life." You can almost feel Paul's heart break as he pens these words.

Let's learn from the unfortunate story of Demas. Don't let love for the things of this life eclipse your love for the Father. Don't let a love for the things of this life cause you to chase after that which is fleeting and passing away. Let the love of the Father found in Jesus come in. Love the Father with all your heart, and see every room you enter become a sanctuary of love from the Father, all your work a sacrifice of love to the Father, and every praise that rolls off your lips a confession of love for the Father. Love the Father supremely who has loved you so deeply. There will be no regrets. God's Word says so.

Reflect and Discuss

1. Why might it be shocking to some to hear that God hates certain things? Why is it important for us not to lose sight of this hatred?
2. Why is it important to reflect on what we have in Christ, as John does in this section?
3. In what sense do believers have victory over the evil one? How does this give you encouragement and hope?
4. What are some ways that worldliness is often misunderstood? How should we understand worldliness, biblically?
5. What are some things we need as God's image-bearers that the world cannot provide?
6. What are some things that the world promises to provide but cannot?
7. Spend some time reflecting on the lusts of the flesh, the desires of the eyes, and pride in possessions. Are there any areas in your life where these temptations are waging war?

8. How does Jesus set an example for how to resist each of these temptations?
9. John argues that the pleasures of this world are fleeting. How do you see this in today's culture? In your own life?
10. How does increasing our love for God help defeat these sinful desires?

The Antichrist(s)

1 JOHN 2:18-27

Main Idea: There have always been those, and more will come, who actively oppose Christ and the gospel; Christians must resist such error and cling to the truth of God as revealed by the Spirit in the Scriptures.

I. **Antichrists Attack Christ (2:18).**
   A. Antichrist has a period of time.
   B. Antichrist is a principle of spiritual error.
   C. Antichrist is a person of deception.
II. **Antichrists Abandon the Church (2:19,22-23).**
   A. Physically, they desert the fellowship (2:19).
   B. Spiritually, they deny the faith (2:22-23).
III. **Antichrists Assault the Christian (2:20-21,24-27).**
   A. We have experienced the anointing of the Spirit (2:20-21,27).
   B. We must embrace the authority of the Scriptures (2:24-26).

One of the earliest and most important lessons we Americans teach our children is how to tell time. This is because we live in a time-conscious culture. Whereas people in many other parts of the world worry much less about deadlines and dates, we are rather obsessed with them. Being early is not fashionable. Being late can often be costly.

The apostle John was also concerned that we know how to tell time. However, it was not *chronological* time-telling that concerned him. It was *spiritual* clock-watching that he deemed of first importance. His interest was not time as man measures it, but time as God measures it. How God reckons time is an important theological issue that should concern the heart and occupy the mind of every follower of Jesus Christ. You see, as God keeps time, "it is the last hour" (v. 18). Time is running out. Midnight is almost here. How do we know this? According to John, unmistakable evidence has appeared: the antichrists have come on the scene!

The word "antichrist" (Gk *antichristos*) has a way of striking a sense of wonder, amazement, and even fear in our hearts. And in one sense it should. Nevertheless, given all the strange and wild speculations that surface when antichrist is mentioned, it is absolutely essential that we have a biblically balanced understanding of *who* the antichrists are and *what* the antichrists do.

In our text John will place before us three important lessons that will equip us to both recognize and defeat these archenemies of the true Christ, our Savior the Lord Jesus. It is time to get armed for the battle. Spiritual conflict is inevitable.

Antichrists Attack Christ
1 JOHN 2:18

The apostle John did not go looking for a fight. However, he would not run from one when those he loved and cared for were in danger of being lied to (v. 22) and deceived (v. 26). Once again he addresses his readers as "children" (cf. vv. 1,12,13). It is a term of endearment and tender affection. It is also a literary device John uses to introduce a new subject. Here, that subject is "the last hour" and the appearance of "many antichrists." The word "antichrist" means "against Christ" or "in the place of Christ." The primary idea in this case is that these enemies are "against Christ." Only John uses this striking term and only in four places in his letters (1 John 2:18,22; 4:3; 2 John 7). While John appears to have coined the word, he did not make up the idea. Daniel calls this rival of Christ "the coming prince" (Dan 9:27). Paul calls him the "man of lawlessness" (2 Thess 2:3). John will picture him as the beast from the sea in Revelation 13:1-10. In this text, John notes several important truths about this spiritual nemesis.

Antichrist Has a Period of Time

John says at the beginning and the end of verse 18, "it is the last hour." It is crucial that we understand what this term means if we are to develop a proper eschatology. Note that John said it was the last hour almost 2,000 years ago. The phrase signifies the entire period of time between the first and second comings of Christ. This is a consistent teaching of the New Testament. Note the following passages:

> *On the contrary, this is what was spoken through the prophet Joel: And it will be in the last days, says God, that I will pour out My Spirit on all humanity; then your sons and your daughters will prophesy, your young men will see visions, and your old men will dream dreams.* (Acts 2:16-17)

Now these things happened to them as examples, and they were written as a warning to us, on whom the ends of the ages have come. (1 Cor 10:11)

But know this: Difficult times will come in the last days. (2 Tim 3:1)

Long ago God spoke to the fathers by the prophets at different times and in different ways. In these last days, He has spoken to us by His Son. God has appointed Him heir of all things and made the universe through Him. (Heb 1:1-2)

Otherwise, He would have had to suffer many times since the foundation of the world. But now He has appeared one time, at the end of the ages, for the removal of sin by the sacrifice of Himself. (Heb 9:26)

He was chosen before the foundation of the world but was revealed at the end of the times for you. (1 Pet 1:20)

The last hour evokes the sense of imminence and urgency in which those who follow Christ must live in throughout any and every age. We live in a time when antichrists (plural) are active. This activity will increase until "the Antichrist" comes at the end of the last hour. Jesus Himself warned us of all of this in Matthew 24:4-5,24-25. As the gospel spreads, so will false teaching. As Christ's missionaries go out to the nations, so will Satan's missionaries called "antichrists"! We are engaged in a global conflict for the souls of men. Interestingly, there could be no antichrists if there was not a true Christ. Even their coming is a witness concerning His coming!

Antichrist Is a Principle of Spiritual Error

In 1 John 4:3 the apostle speaks of "the spirit of the antichrist." In our text in 2:22, he makes plain what the spirit of antichrist is all about: they are liars who deny "that Jesus is the Messiah." And their strategy is deceptive and seductive. They do not directly oppose Jesus Christ. They redefine Him. They re-imagine Him. "He is good," they say, "but He is not God." "He may be a son of God like we can be sons and daughters of God," they teach, "but He is not *the* Son of God." "He may have died on the cross as a martyr," they affirm, "but He did not die as a Savior." The spirit of antichrist always diminishes the person and work of Christ. It chips away at His deity and rejects His work of atonement. The antichrist spirit thinks and then teaches incorrectly concerning *who* Jesus Christ is and *what* Jesus Christ has done. The "hub" of Christianity is the person and work of Jesus of Nazareth, the eternal and divine Son of God. If you get it wrong here, you will get it wrong almost everywhere else. This is the spirit of the antichrists, and it will attempt to lead you down the road of spiritual error that is a theological dead end.

Antichrist Is a Person of Deception

John makes an important distinction between many antichrists who are already here and the Antichrist who is coming at the end of the age. Satan's superman will appear someday. The Devil's darling will make a grand entrance sometime in the future. This counterfeit Christ will come on the scene of world history and, amazingly, the whole earth will marvel and follow him. Satan will indwell him and give him "his power, his throne, and great authority" (Rev 13:2-3). The Bible teaches that the nations will even worship him as God (Rev 13:4).

Now you may ask, "When is he coming? Could he be alive right now?" Several years ago *Newsweek* reported that 19 percent of all Americans and 50 percent of those who accept biblical prophecy believe the antichrist is alive today (Woodward, "The Way the World Ends," 69). Whether he is alive or not, I cannot, will not, and should not speculate, and neither should you. That is God's business. What I do know is he will come, and the spirit of antichrist is alive and well. So, be on the lookout for those who attack the biblical teachings about Christ. They will do you no good.

Antichrists Abandon the Church
1 JOHN 2:19,22-23

The greatest dangers to the church of the Lord Jesus Christ are always from within, not from without. Satan is a master deceiver and strategist who knows that the deployment of a spiritual Trojan Horse can do serious, if not irreparable, damage to the body of Christ. However, once the damage is done, the antichrists will leave the spiritual battlefield taking with them what captives they can. Eventually they reveal their true colors and allegiance. Their departure will almost always be painful and the occasion for tremendous grief. But their exit is essential for the health and vitality of the church. Alistair Begg says it well: "There are some who share [for a while] our earthly company who do not share our heavenly birth" ("A Word of Warning"). You see, their leaving us is a clear sign and certain signal that they were really never a part of us to begin with.

Physically, They Desert the Fellowship (1 John 2:19)

Perseverance is the proof of possession. Defection from the fellowship gives evidence of a defective faith. That was certainly John's perspective.

The contrast between "they" and "us" in verse 19 is striking. In the original text both words appear five times. There are two spiritual teams as John sees it. There is "us" and there is "them" (they). Several observations can be made about each team. First, the "they team" did not last. They left. "They went out from us." Most likely this was a voluntary departure not an excommunication, though both are certainly possible. Second, their departure proves they were never really a part of us regardless of what they once professed. In other words they were never truly saved; they never truly experienced the new birth of regeneration (cf. 2:29; 3:9; 4:7; 5:4,9-10,18). They were and are lost.

The "us team" in contrast remains in the fellowship and perseveres. As tragic as this verse is on one hand, it is glorious and comforting on the other. Why? Because it is a wonderful affirmation of what we call "eternal security" or "perseverance of the saints." Those who truly belong to Christ will stay with Christ because, as Jude 1 says, we are "kept for Jesus Christ." Jesus addressed this wonderful truth in John 10:27-29 where He says, "My sheep hear My voice, I know them, and they follow Me. I give them eternal life, and they will never perish—ever! No one will snatch them out of My hand. My Father, who has given them to Me, is greater than all. No one is able to snatch them out of the Father's hand." I love what the Baptist Faith and Message 2000 says of this doctrine in Article V on "God's Purpose of Grace": "All true believers endure to the end. Those whom God has accepted in Christ, and sanctified by His Spirit, will never fall away from the state of grace, but shall persevere to the end. Believers may fall into sin through neglect and temptation, whereby they grieve the Spirit, impair their graces and comforts, and bring reproach on the cause of Christ and temporal judgments on themselves; yet they shall be kept by the power of God through faith unto salvation."

Spiritually, They Deny the Faith (1 John 2:22-23)

The physical desertion of the false teachers and their disciples was grounded in their defection from and denial of the faith. They left the church because they had left Christ. They no longer believed what the apostles, those who had been with Him, taught. They denied the incarnation and deity of Christ, that Jesus was the One sent by the Father. And their rejection of the biblical and apostolic witness concerning Jesus was personally tragic and spiritually disastrous. You see, to deny the Son is to deny His Father who sent Him. This is a package deal, as verses 22-23 make crystal clear. Indeed, "No one who denies the Son can have the Father." But, and this is good news, "He who confesses the Son has the Father as well."

Once again we see the Christological test is the crucial test. What do you think and believe about Jesus Christ? To these heretics, and that is what they were, Jesus was *important* but not *preeminent*. He was *significant* but not the *Savior*. However, the New Testament scholar I. H. Marshall is right on target when he says, "To deny that Jesus is the Christ is to deny that He is the Son of God" (*The Epistles of John*, 158). He further notes,

> To reduce Jesus to the status of a mere man, or to allow no more than a temporary indwelling of some divine power in Him is to strike at the root of Christianity. Modern thinkers may have more refined ways of stating similar denials of the reality of the incarnation. It may be doubted whether they are any more immune to John's perception that they take the heart out of Christianity. (*The Epistles of John*, 159)

Friedrich Schleiermacher (1768–1834), the father of modern liberal theology, offered an adoptionist understanding of Jesus, dismissing as outrageous the idea that Jesus was the eternal Son of God who became human. What distinguished Jesus from other humans was "the constant potency of His God-consciousness, which was a veritable existence of God in Him" (Schleiermacher, *The Christian Faith*, 385). Jesus was a God-filled man, a God-intoxicated man, but not the God-man. Liberal theologian John Macquarrie says, "Jesus Christ pre-existed in the mind and purpose of God, and I doubt if one should look for any other kind of pre-existence" (*Jesus Christ in Modern Thought*, 57). And religious pluralist John Hick says, "We see in Jesus a human being extraordinarily open to God's influence and thus living to an extraordinary extent as God's agent on earth, 'incarnating' the divine purpose for human life.

He thus embodied . . . the ideal of humanity living in openness and response to God, and in doing so He 'incarnated' a love that reflects the divine love" (*The Metaphor of God Incarnate*, 12).

Sadly, many of these modern false teachers and others like them have left the faith but have sought to remain in the fellowship. Their deadly poison continues to infect the body of Christ with its lies. John has given us a way to identify them. We must have the courage to expose them, even though it hurts to do so. It is always better to be divided by truth than united by error.

Antichrists Assault the Christian
1 JOHN 2:20-21,24-27

The proliferation of the antichrists, these false teachers, could easily discourage us. They are, after all, intellectual heavyweights with persuasive arguments and personalities. And as John makes clear, they are committed to our defeat. However, we should not despair. First John 4:4 promises us, "You are from God, little children, and you have conquered them, because the One who is in you is greater than the one who is in the world." John reminds us that we have a twofold arsenal that Satan, the antichrists, the liars and deceivers cannot withstand. One is the anointing of the Spirit. The other is the Word of God. "Word and Spirit" was the battle cry of the Protestant Reformation as the Reformers recaptured the truth of "justification by faith alone in Christ alone for the glory of God alone." I believe Word and Spirit must also be the battle cry of every generation of those who follow Jesus if they are to abide in the Son and in the Father (v. 24).

We Have Experienced the Anointing of the Spirit
(1 John 2:20-21,27)

What has enabled us to remain in the apostles' teaching and the community of faith (v. 19)? We have "an anointing from the Holy One" (v. 20). "You have" is emphatic and draws a stark contrast with the antichrists of 2:18-19. This anointing refers to our receiving the Holy Spirit (cf. John 14:17; 15:26; 16:13; 1 Cor 1:21). The "Holy One" who provides this anointing is probably Jesus, who is referred to by this title numerous times in Scripture (Mark 1:24; Luke 4:34; John 6:69; Acts 3:14; Rev 3:7). However, that the Godhead in general is in view should not be ruled out. Consecrated and set apart by God and for God by the Holy Spirit, we now have an internal and abiding Teacher who will guide us in all knowledge and truth (vv. 21,27). And, by abiding in Him, no lie will seduce us, deceive us, and lead us astray.

Some have been troubled by these verses, especially verse 27, which seems to imply that having been given the Spirit, we now need no human teachers. What are we to make of this? The Bible consistently advocates teaching (Matt 28:20; 1 Cor 12:28; Eph 4:11; Col 3:16; 1 Tim 4:11; 2 Tim 2:2,24). Therefore, we can confidently say that John is not ruling out a human teacher. The fact that he wrote this letter makes that clear! Instead, this is what he is getting at: At the time he wrote, the antichrists, the false teachers, were insisting that the teaching of the apostles was to be supplemented with an additional "higher knowledge," an "advanced knowledge," that they claimed to possess. John's response was that what the readers were taught under the Spirit's ministry through the apostles was not only adequate, it was the only reliable truth. The teaching ministry of the Holy Spirit (what we call "illumination") does not involve revelation of new truth. Rather, it is the enablement to appropriate God's truth that has already been revealed. All things necessary for salvation are ours; we need nothing more. Let the Holy Spirit be your guide, not another spirit.

We Must Embrace the Authority of the Scriptures (1 John 2:24-26)

John now reintroduces a concept that is one of his favorites: *abiding*. He will use this term (Gk *meno*, translated to English as "abide" or "remain") 23 times in 1 John, seven of which appear in 2:18-28. It conveys the ideas of both union and communion. John says you should abide in the Word you have received in Christ. In verse 24, John challenges the believer to simply remain in the teaching of Christ that they had received at the beginning, at conversion. To abide and remain in this teaching is to abide and remain in both the Son and the Father. There is not any additional thing you need. Jesus plus nothing equals everything (Tchividjian, *Jesus + Nothing = Everything*). Jesus plus something extra equals heresy and the teachings of the antichrist. All you need is Christ, and with Christ comes the Father too. Further, it is only in the Son sent by the Father that the gift of eternal life is promised. This is a promise made by God (v. 25), a promise that can never be broken.

The false teachers will attempt to deceive you into thinking you need something more than Christ or something other than Christ. They are liars (vv. 22,27). The Spirit and the apostles' teaching (the Word) always agree. If what men teach goes against or beyond what those who knew Jesus taught, mark them because they are not of God. They have a different spirit, the spirit of antichrist.

Conclusion

Herman Bavinck was a Dutch churchman and theologian in the late nineteenth and early twentieth centuries. He also was an insightful teacher concerning the person and work of Christ. Concerning the centrality of Christ to the Christian gospel, he simply and concisely said, "Christ is Christianity itself; He stands not outside of it but in its centre; without His name, person and work, there is no Christianity left. In a word, Christ does not point out the way to salvation; He is the Way itself" (quoted in Warfield, *The Person and Work of Christ*, 319). This is what the apostles taught. This is what the Word says. This is what the Spirit affirms. This is what we believe. This is where we abide. This is what we confess. Eternal life is what we are promised!

Reflect and Discuss

1. Antichrist has only a period of time. When is that time? How does this truth encourage you toward faithfulness?
2. Why is it important to remember that Antichrist is both a principle and a person? How can we identify the principle around us?
3. What are the dangers of too much speculation about the person John identifies as "Antichrist"? How can we keep a biblical perspective on looking out for this person?
4. Why don't antichrists remain in the fellowship of the church? Why do true believers remain in the fellowship?
5. Doctrinally, how can we identify the spirit of antichrist?
6. Using the Christological test, how do we identify true believers? What have been some heretical answers throughout Church history?
7. Why is it important to expose false teachers in the church? What is the best way to do this?
8. How can we use both Word and Spirit in the fight against the spirit of antichrist?
9. What is the role of human teachers in the church, since all believers have been given the Spirit of God?

The Blessings of Abiding In Jesus

1 JOHN 2:28–3:3

Main Idea: True believers will remain in fellowship with Christ and experience the blessings that come through communion with Him.

I. You Will Be Confident at His Coming (2:28).
II. You Will Be Certain You Are His Child (2:29–3:1).
III. You Will Be Conformed to Christ (3:2).
IV. You Will Be Consistent in Your Consecration (3:3).

In recent days we have rediscovered one of my favorite gospel hymns. The words were written by a well-known Presbyterian evangelist of the late nineteenth century named John Wilber Chapman (1859–1918). The song is titled "One Day." Casting Crowns has popularized it once again with the title "Glorious Day." Telling the wonderful drama of redemption, verse 5 brings the story to its climactic conclusion with these words concerning King Jesus:

> One day the trumpet will sound for His coming,
> One day the skies with His glory will shine;
> Wonderful day, my beloved ones bringing;
> Glorious Savior, this Jesus is mine!

Then the refrain:

> Living He loved me; dying He saved me;
> Buried, He carried my sins far away;
> Rising He justified freely forever;
> One day He's coming—Oh glorious day!

That glorious day is indeed coming and the apostle John sees it as an awesome hope for the future and a powerful motivation for the present. Because I am going to be like Him in the future and for all eternity, such a promise has a wonderful transforming power in the present. My future impacts my life today!

In 1 John 2:28–3:3, God's Word tells us we are destined to look like, think like, talk like, act like, and be like Jesus (3:2). As God's sons and daughters through the new birth (2:29–3:2), we have a future hope that, in one sense, cannot be put into words. John is so honest when he writes, "What we will be has not yet been revealed" (3:2). However, what we do know, as we abide in Jesus, is more than enough!

John, as a loving spiritual father, has given his "little children" (2:1,12,18,28) a number of words of challenge and encouragement up until this point in his letter. He has encouraged them to find full joy in fellowship with the Father and the Son (1:1-4). He has called them to walk in the light of God and stay close to Christ (1:5–2:2). They are to do this by obeying the Lord's commands and by loving others (2:3-11). They must also know their spiritual status and not be seduced by the world (2:12-17). Likewise, they must beware of the enemies of the faith who deny Jesus is the Messiah (2:18-27). Now in the present text he adds the exhortation to abide in Christ and pursue a righteous life as they live in the hope of His coming (2:28–3:3). In other words, as Christians, what we are going to be then will transform the way we live today! In fact, such a spiritual posture will result in four wonderful blessings—blessings that are promised to everyone who keeps on abiding in Christ.

You Will Be Confident at His Coming
1 JOHN 2:28

John again addresses his readers with the tender term "little children." And he continues the theme of remaining or abiding in Christ, which was a key concern in 2:18-27 and an essential protection against false teaching. The word "remain" is a present imperative. It is a word of command and calls for consistent action. Remain in union and communion with Christ. Soak in the Savior and the gospel message that you heard at the beginning of your Christian experience (2:24).

I believe both salvation and sanctification are on John's radar screen as he encourages us to stay with Jesus. And abiding brings with it a wonderful companion: assurance, which is confidence at the second coming of the Lord Jesus. Here is John's point: Christ is coming again. He will appear on this earth again officially and in full public display as King of kings and Lord over all lords. So, "when He appears" (Gk *parousia*), will you "have boldness" or will you "be ashamed before Him"? Will you run toward Him as a child runs to a loving father, or will you draw back and attempt to hide from His glorious, regal coming?

Is it possible to be saved and yet ashamed when you stand before
Jesus? I think the answer has to be yes. Paul seems to address the
possibility in 1 Corinthians 3:15 when, at the judgment seat of Christ,
he says some will have their works burned up because their foundation
was "wood, hay, or straw" (1 Cor 3:12). Yes, "it will be lost, but he will be
saved; yet it will be like an escape through fire."

But there is another question begging to be asked: Might John be
addressing those who are "ashamed before Him at his coming" because
they are lost? This may be what John is really saying. After all, in Mark
8:38 Jesus said,

> For whoever is ashamed of Me and of My words in this adulterous and
> sinful generation, the Son of Man will also be ashamed of him when
> He comes in the glory of His Father with the holy angels.

And in Revelation 6:15-16 we read these terrifying words:

> Then the kings of the earth, the nobles, the military commanders,
> the rich, the powerful, and every slave and free person hid in the
> caves and among the rocks of the mountains. And they said to the
> mountains and to the rocks, "Fall on us and hide us from the face of
> the One seated on the throne and from the wrath of the Lamb."

Reflect on your reaction to seeing Jesus at His second coming. It can
be very revealing in terms of your spiritual status and health. This much
I do know: He wants you to have the confidence of a child jumping into
the arms of a loving daddy. He doesn't want you running to a closet or
cave, hiding in shame.

You Will Be Certain You Are His Child
1 JOHN 2:29–3:1

In Revelation 19:11-21 we have a full and majestic description of
Christ's second coming. In verse 11 it says, "He judges and makes
war in righteousness." The coming King is also a righteous King. We
already saw this in 1 John 2:1. And because He is righteous, one thing
is certain: "Everyone who does what is right has been born of Him"
(2:29). Here, John uses what I call a root/fruit argument, noting what
we see before addressing why we see it. He tells us that the fruit of
doing what is right reveals that in our roots, i.e., our hearts, we have
been born again.

The new birth precedes new behavior. Being born of God has definite and abiding results ("has been born" is a perfect-tense verb). Therefore, children of God will grow to look like God their Father. Our practice is proof of our parentage. The righteous Savior produces righteous saints.

John carries this argument an additional step in 3:1, and what a step it is! He explains how the love of God the Father is the source of our privilege to be His children. Calling their attention to this wonderful truth, he exclaims, "Look at how great a love the Father has given us!" What John says could be paraphrased like this: "The love of the Father is out of this world and it is a love that will never be taken away. It is an amazing love that awes and astonishes, and it has been given for us to enjoy forever and ever and ever." Hebrews 13:5 is really true: "I will never leave you or forsake you."

This Father's love is a forever-love and its results are twofold: (1) We are now called the children of God, and (2) this is truly who we are! That we are called His children means we bear His name. That we are His children means we have His nature. Once I was a slave to sin but now I am a child of God. What an amazing truth to grasp and meditate on. What a beautiful balance this brings to my self-awareness. There is no place for either an inferiority or a superiority complex. I am who I am by gracious adoption and regeneration. That fosters humility. I am who I am as God's child. That fosters security and certainty.

Let me give just one example of how this should impact a couple of important relationships. One is dating and the other is marriage. When I was dating my wife Charlotte, I was *dating* God's daughter. Whatever her earthly father thought of my treatment of her pales in comparison to what her heavenly Father thought! Today, I am *married* to God's daughter. Although the status of our relationship changed at marriage, He remains vitally interested in how I take care of His little girl! That affects the way I love and serve her as my wife!

In almost a passing comment, John says this world doesn't understand this remarkable relationship. This truth should not really surprise us. After all, "It didn't know Him" (3:1). Therefore, it will not know, understand, or appreciate those who know Him and are increasingly becoming like Him. Jesus told us to expect all of this when He said in John 15:18-19,

> *If the world hates you, understand that it hated Me before it hated you. If you were of the world, the world would love you as its own. However,*

*because you are not of the world, but I have chosen you out of it, the
world hates you.*

The world did not really understand Him 2,000 years ago. Don't be surprised when the world does not really understand us today. It should be
expected.

You Will Be Conformed to Christ
1 JOHN 3:2

Our salvation through the gospel of Jesus Christ is more than a rescue.
It is a complete and total renovation—or better, transformation—that
transcends what any human words can describe. This becomes evident
in what we can know and what we cannot know in verse 2. First, we can
know we are loved ("Beloved" ESV or "Dear friends" HCSB) and that we
are God's sons and daughters right now, this very moment. I am in the
fullest sense the one God created me to be and the one He redeemed
me to be through the new birth (cf. 2:29; 3:9-10). Second, what we will
ultimately be is not completely known to us at the present time.

There is a tension in our Christian experience that theologians
often refer to as the "already/not yet" of Christian salvation. We are
already, today, children of God. However, we do not yet realize or
experience all the benefits that salvation promises for God's children.
We are still in process, a work under construction, a divine work of art
that is not yet complete. We cannot even imagine the glory in store for
us. First Corinthians 2:9 puts it like this: "What eye did not see and ear
did not hear, and what never entered the human mind—God prepared
this for those who love Him." First Corinthians 13:12 adds, "For now we
see indistinctly, as in a mirror, but then face to face. Now I know in part,
but then I will know fully, as I am fully known."

This leads to a third observation, and one of the most amazing
truths in the whole Bible: "We know that when He appears, we will be
like Him because we will see Him as He is." Praise the Lord! John's
"apostolic ignorance" now gives way to theological amazement. We shall
be like Him! As Jonathan Edwards said, "Grace is glory begun, and glory
is grace completed" (Edwards and James, "Growth in Grace," 56). The
perfection of God's grace will be realized in our full, complete, total,
and permanent glorification. Psalm 17:15 says it so beautifully: "But I
will see Your face in righteousness; when I awake, I will be satisfied with
Your presence." Romans 8:29 teaches us that we are being conformed to

the image of Jesus, and 1 John 3:2 tells us it will reach that intended goal when we see Him as He is, as the resurrected and glorified King of glory. William Alexander tells the story that when native converts came to this phrase as they were translating the Bible into their language, they laid down their pens and exclaimed "No! it is too much . . . let us write that we shall be permitted to kiss His feet'" (Cook, 326). But surely it is true. We will see Him face to face, and we will be conformed to His image.

We don't know all that being made like Jesus means. What we do know is it will be better than we could ever hope or imagine, and it will be the occasion for an eternal lifetime of praise, worship, and adoration.

You Will Be Consistent in Your Consecration
1 JOHN 3:3

First John 3:2 is the very definition of Christian hope, and 1 John 3:3 is the natural response to that hope. Every one of us who has this hope in us, the hope of someday being like Jesus, cannot help but respond in a very specific manner. In fact we are delighted to do so. This hope is the confident certainty that God is going to conform me to the exact image of His Son, and consequently it motivates me to continually pursue a life of purity and holiness, just as Jesus is pure and holy. Eugene Peterson in *The Message* says it like this: "All of us who look forward to his Coming stay ready, with the glistening purity of Jesus' life as a model for our own."

The word *pure* means "free from contamination" and is used of ceremonial cleansings (John 11:55), cleansing of the heart (Jas 4:8), and even cleansing of the soul (1 Pet 1:22). Here it is used in reference to one's total life. My hope for the future enables me to pursue holiness in the present. Being heavenly minded actually makes me fit for earthly good. Paul said the same thing in Colossians 3:1-4 where he writes,

> So if you have been raised with the Messiah, seek what is above, where the Messiah is, seated at the right hand of God. Set your minds on what is above, not on what is on the earth. For you have died, and your life is hidden with the Messiah in God. When the Messiah, who is your life, is revealed, then you also will be revealed with Him in glory.

Pastor Sam Storms is exactly right in his understanding of how our vision of Christ ties into our sanctification: "Just as the vision of Christ in the future will sanctify us wholly, the vision of Christ in the present (in

Scripture) sanctifies us progressively. It is our experience of Christ that sanctifies" (Storms, "First John 2:28–3:3"). Isn't it great to know, as Paul wrote in Philippians 1:6, that "He who started a good work in you will carry it on to completion until the day of Christ Jesus"?

Conclusion

I began our study with a song. Let me close with one too. It was written by Frances Jane "Fanny" Crosby (1820–1915). She was an American rescue mission worker and songwriter who penned more than 8,000 hymns. And she was blind. That is why one of her most popular songs is all the more remarkable. Its title: "Blessed Assurance, Jesus is Mine." In the context of 1 John 2:28–3:3, stanzas 1 and 3 really stand out.

> Blessed assurance, Jesus is mine!
> Oh, what a foretaste of glory divine!
> Heir of salvation, purchase of God,
> Born of His Spirit, washed in His blood.

> Perfect submission, all is at rest,
> I in my Savior am happy and blest:
> Watching and waiting, looking above,
> Filled with His goodness, lost in His love.

Just as Fanny Crosby was, in her blindness, "watching and waiting," we must likewise set our eyes on the hope we have, that we will one day see His face and be like Him. These are just some of the blessings of abiding in Christ. If this is so, why would you want to abide anywhere else but in Jesus?!

Reflect and Discuss

1. Why is "abiding" important in the Christian life? How is abiding different from "getting saved"?
2. How do you think you will react when you first see Jesus revealed in all His glory? What are some things that might cause someone to be ashamed at His appearing?
3. What is a root/fruit argument and how is it important for the Christian life? What other passages of Scripture use similar logic?
4. How does knowing that all Christians are God's children affect your relationship with the following: (a) spouse, (b) parent/child, (c) church member, (d) the world?

5. What does it mean for the world to not know Christ? How will that affect our relationship with the world?

6. Why is it such a blessing to know that abiding believers will be conformed to Christ's image?

7. How can a promise of seeing Jesus inspire Christians to pursue holiness? Why is holiness the natural response to Christian hope?

Why Did the Son of God Invade Planet Earth?

1 JOHN 3:4-10

Main Idea: Jesus Christ came to redeem and renew sinners by paying the penalty of sin and defeating the Devil.

I. **He Came to Deliver Us from Sin (3:4-6).**
   A. Christ appeared and dealt with sin (3:4-5).
   B. Christians abide in Christ and do not live in sin (3:6).
II. **He Came to Destroy the Works of the Devil (3:7-8).**
   A. The Devil is a deceiver, so pursue righteousness (3:7).
   B. The Devil is a sinner who has been defeated (3:8).
III. **He Came to Demarcate the Children of God (3:9-10).**
   A. God's children have experienced a new birth (3:9).
   B. God's children do not practice sin (3:9).
   C. God's children love one another (3:10).

As the storm clouds of World War II were approaching, German Pastor Dietrich Bonhoeffer preached a sermon on November 26, 1939, entitled "Death Is Swallowed Up in Victory." He brought his message to a close with these words:

> When dark hours and when the darkest hour comes over us, then we want to hear the voice of Jesus Christ calling in our ear: *victory is won.* Death is swallowed up in victory. Take comfort. And may God grant that then we will be able to say: I believe in the forgiveness of sins, the resurrection of the body, and the life everlasting. It is in this faith that we want to live and die. (Bonhoeffer, *The Collected Sermons*, 210; emphasis in original)

While his text on that occasion came from 1 Corinthians 15, his words surely resonate with these verses in 1 John, which remind us that Jesus Christ appeared in order both to take away our sins (3:5) and to destroy the works of the Devil (v. 8). We can indeed hear the voice of Jesus in this text calling in our ear: "Victory is won."

John has informed us that we have been born of God and are now His children (2:29–3:2). He also taught us that the practice of righteousness provides evidence that one is a child of God. Now he proceeds to show how being a child of God is incompatible with the practice of sin. The two simply do not go together. They are enemies to the death. John has challenged us to live a life of righteousness (2:29) and purity (3:3) grounded in the promise of the second coming of Christ. Now John gives the same challenge based on His first coming (3:5,8). John Stott puts it in proper perspective:

> If Christ appeared first both to "take away our sins" and to "destroy the devil's work," and if, when he appears a second time, "we shall see him" and, in consequence, "we shall be like him," how can we possibly go on living in sin? To do so would be to deny the purpose of both his "appearings." (*The Letters of John*, 132–33)

Thus, His "two comings" serve as theological and eschatological bookends to inspire and motivate us to "walk just as He walked" (2:6), to do what is right (2:29; 3:7,10), to purify ourselves (3:3), and to love our brother (3:10) as we abide in Him (3:6,9).

Thabiti Anyabwile points out that the apostle John addresses basically four different groups of people in his letters. They are: (1) fully assured Christians; (2) Christians struggling with assurance; (3) falsely assured non-Christians; and (4) known non-Christians (unpublished sermon notes). These verses are, of course, for all of us. But John especially has the third group in his sights here. His goal is to shock them and wake them up to their true spiritual status.

He Came to Deliver Us from Sin
1 JOHN 3:4-6

Sin is the great enemy and problem of humanity, and only God can rescue us and solve our problem. That is one reason that when I teach Bible interpretation, I always teach my students to ask two questions as they begin to examine a passage. First, they should ask, "What does this text teach me about God (His character and ways)?" Second, they should ask, "What does this text teach me about fallen, sinful humanity (that requires the grace of God)?" John addresses both of these questions in verses 4-6, though he will do it in reverse order. First he notes the problem. Then he provides the solution.

Christ Appeared and Dealt with Sin (1 John 3:4-5)

There is a universal truth John sets before us in verse 4: "Everyone who commits sin also breaks the law; sin is the breaking of law." Sin is lawlessness, rebellion, a defiant disregard and rejection of God's rightful rule as Lord over your life. In your practice of sin, you rebel against your rightful King and say, "I hate Your law." Sin is nothing less than personal treason against the Sovereign of the universe. And sin is not a one-time offense. It is the habitual and settled disposition of your heart and your life that makes you, as Anyabwile says, "an outlaw against God" (unpublished sermon notes).

Because our predicament is so great, a great rescue is required. We know this is why Christ came in the incarnation: "He was revealed so that He might take away sins" (v. 5). Can't you hear John the Baptist at the Jordan River, heralding to the top of his lungs, "Here is the Lamb of God, who takes away the sin of the world!" (John 1:29)? By His bloody death on the cross, Jesus lifted up, removed, and carried away our sins. The Son of God came to provide full and everlasting forgiveness of sins to all who trust in Him.

And do not miss this: He could do what He did because He is who He is. "There is no sin in Him" (v. 5). Not even one! His sinlessness is part of what qualified Him to provide the needed rescue, which is why His lack of sin is a consistent theme that resounds throughout the Bible. John himself has already taught us He is the righteous one (2:29) and the pure one (3:3). Now he explicitly identifies Jesus as the sinless one. Paul agrees, for in 2 Corinthians 5:21 he writes, "He made the One who did not know sin to be sin for us, so that we might become the righteousness of God in Him." The author of Hebrews also agrees. In Hebrews 4:15 he tells us, "For we do not have a high priest who is unable to sympathize with our weaknesses, but One who has been tested in every way as we are, yet without sin." Again in Hebrews 7:25-26 he says, "Therefore, He is always able to save those who come to God through Him, since He always lives to intercede for them. For this is the kind of high priest we need: holy, innocent, undefiled, separated from sinners, and exalted above the heavens." Peter also agrees, because in 1 Peter 2:22 he writes, "He did not commit sin, and no deceit was found in His mouth." Christ has indeed appeared, lived a sinless life, and dealt with our sin. All of Scripture testifies to this truth.

Christians Abide in Christ and Do Not Live in Sin (1 John 3:6)

Verse 6 logically and necessarily flows from verse 5. Because there is no sin in Jesus, no one who abides in Him keeps on sinning. In fact, if one does continue in a pattern or practice of sin, another logical and necessary conclusion must be drawn: "everyone who sins [keeps on sinning] has not seen Him or known Him" in a personal, saving relationship. John's theology is flawless. If the sinless Son of God appeared in history to take away sin, how is it possible to abide in Him and sin at the same time? The answer is, you can't. It is impossible.

Some have understood verses 6 and 9 to affirm sinless perfection in this life. This, however, would contradict what John said in 1:8,10. No, the use of the present tense verb in verses 6 and 9 help us see what John is saying. Because of the new birth, we have a new nature. Because Christ has taken away our sins, we have a new liberty and freedom. Sin no longer dominates us or enslaves us. Sin is no longer the character and conduct of my life. Because I now abide in Christ and in the power of His person and work in the gospel, I may fall into sin, but I will not walk in sin. Sin will not be my habit; it will not be my normal practice. I no longer love sin; I hate sin. I no longer delight in sin; I despise sin.

In my union with Christ, which is another way of saying abiding in Christ, I have experienced a definite and decisive break with sin. It no longer rules me. Christ does! A life of living in sin and living in the Savior is an oxymoron. It does not make sense. It is spiritually absurd.

He Came to Destroy the Works of the Devil
1 JOHN 3:7-8

If sin is personal enemy number one, then Satan is public enemy number one. The flesh is our internal foe and the Devil is our external foe. We now, in Christ, wage a titanic spiritual war on two fronts. But do not fear or be discouraged. The Warrior Lamb (Rev 5) who defeated sin is also our champion who has defeated Satan. The Devil is doomed, even if he won't admit it! False teachers are behind the lie that one can be born of God, born again, and still practice a lifestyle of sin. And behind the false teachers is the father of lies himself, the Devil (John 8:44).

The Devil Is a Deceiver, So Pursue Righteousness (1 John 3:7)

Getting confused and wrongheaded about the seriousness of sin can be a serious spiritual problem, especially when satanic sirens of our age sing that sin is no big deal. John, therefore, with fatherly firmness ("Little children"), warns his spiritual children against being deceived. "Let no one deceive you" is a present imperative. It is a word of command calling for persistent vigilance. It echoes the prior warning of 2:26: "I have written these things to you about those who are trying to deceive you." Deception can take many forms. In particular, it can trap us both *doctrinally* and *morally*—believing wrongly about the Savior and living wrongly in a lifestyle of sin. It can also capture us *socially* when we fail to love others as we have been loved by God (3:10).

John provides a counter-argument to such deception that is quite simple and to the point: "The one who does what is right is righteous, just as He is righteous." Deception is defeated by a righteous life that gives tangible, visible evidence that we have been born again through faith in Christ. We will live out who we are. It is inevitable. Now, doing what is right is not what enables us to be righteous, but again, it is proof that we are righteous, just as Jesus, in whom we now abide, is righteous.

Christ is my righteousness *positionally* and *experientially*—determining what I am in the eyes of God and directing how I act here on earth. He is my redemption and my sanctification. Christ is my pattern (2:6) and my power (4:4) for righteous living. Galatians 2:19-20 provides a very helpful insight on this truth: "I have been crucified with Christ and I no longer live, but Christ lives in me. The life I now live in the body, I live by faith in the Son of God, who loved me and gave Himself for me." Do not be deceived into thinking you can practice sin and be righteous before God. That is a great, big, satanic lie!

The Devil Is a Sinner Who Has Been Defeated (1 John 3:8)

Verse 8 is one of the clearest statements in all of God's Word telling us why Christ came. For the first time in the letter, John refers specifically and directly to our archenemy the Devil (cf. 3:12; also 2:13-14; 5:18-19). The word "*Devil*" (*diabolos*) appears four times in verses 8-10 and means "accuser or slanderer." "Satan," the Hebrew counterpart, means "adversary." These words well describe the character and tactics of our ancient foe. Jesus came on the scene to take away sin (v. 5) and also "to destroy the Devil's works."

In verse 8 Jesus is referred to as the "Son of God" (the first of seven occurrences in 1 John; see 3:8; 4:15; 5:5,10,12,13,20). The Second Person of the triune God invaded enemy territory and took our enemy down in a complete and total victory. John Piper says, "Christmas is because God aims to destroy something . . . [it is] God's infiltration of rebel planet earth on a search and destroy mission" ("The Son of God Appeared"). He came, searched out, and destroyed the works of Satan. He blew him up!

Seeing verse 8 in parallel with verse 5, we see that the works of the Devil, which our Savior came to destroy, are sins. By means of His atonement, sin's *penalty* has been nullified for the child of God. By means of the new birth, sin's *power* has been neutralized and dealt a death-blow. And, by virtue of His two appearings, sin's *presence* will soon pass away forever. Jesus delivered a knockout punch to the Devil on the cross. An empty tomb is an eternal monument to His victory and to ours!

He Came to Demarcate the Children of God
1 JOHN 3:9-10

As we have seen, the false teachers of John's day, as well as those of our own, will teach that it is possible—someway, somehow—to be righteous without doing what is right. God's Word says, "No way!" Those abiding in Christ will not, indeed they cannot, go on living in sin as the consistent and prevailing pattern of their lives. "Impossible," says the Bible. It simply is not in the realm of reality. Conversion changes everything. Regeneration does not produce invisible or rotten fruit. If anyone is in Christ, he or she is a new creation and all things become new (2 Cor 5:17).

As John closes out this paragraph, he highlights three crystal clear and definite descriptions of the children of God. Being a good teacher, he again uses a little repetition to make sure his children get his point.

God's Children Have Experienced a New Birth (1 John 3:9)

Once more John draws attention to the new birth, to the doctrine of regeneration. One of the distinguishing marks of the Christian is the new birth. He has been converted, born again, regenerated. What is regeneration? What does being born of God mean? The Baptist Faith and Message 2000 says,

Regeneration, or the new birth, is a work of God's grace
whereby believers become new creatures in Christ Jesus. It is a
change of heart wrought by the Holy Spirit through conviction
of sin, to which the sinner responds in repentance toward God
and faith in the Lord Jesus Christ. Repentance and faith are
inseparable experiences of grace. Repentance is a genuine
turning from sin toward God. Faith is the acceptance of Jesus
Christ and commitment of the entire personality to Him as
Lord and Savior.

The *New Bible Dictionary* says regeneration is "a drastic act on fallen
human nature by the Holy Spirit, leading to a change in the person's
whole outlook. He can now be described as a new man who seeks, finds
and follows God in Christ" (Gordon, "Regeneration," 1005).

John teaches us that this happens because God's "seed remains in
him," in the believer. Various views are held concerning what is meant
by God's "seed." They include the Holy Spirit, the Word of God, Christ,
God Himself, and the new nature. In a sense, all are true, though the
new nature specifically seems to fit John's purposes here best. Perhaps
we could say that by means of the work of Christ, revealed in the gospel
message, the Holy Spirit imparts a new nature into everyone who repents
of sin and trusts in Christ. I have no doubt John would affirm this thesis.

God's Children Do Not Practice Sin (1 John 3:9)

Without the new birth it is impossible for us to live like new people. Sin
will dominate us. Satan will have his way with us. Hate and not love will
fill our hearts. However, as a result of the new birth, the Bible says we
cannot make "a practice of sinning" and we "cannot keep on sinning
because [we have] been born of God" (v. 9 ESV). These are words that
should impart both comfort and humility to us. We are comforted to
know sin cannot and will not win, ultimately, in our lives. We may stumble, even fall on occasion, but we know "the One who is in [us] is greater
than the one who is in the world" (4:4). Our Lord will pick us up and get
us moving again in the right direction. We are destined to be like Jesus
(3:2; cf. Rom 8:29-30)! Neither sin nor Satan will have the last word.

These words also humble us because if it were not for Christ, His
atonement, His advocacy, and His victory, we would forever be enslaved
to Satan and sin. Any righteousness we do flows from the righteousness
of Christ poured into our lives by means of the new birth.

God's Children Love One Another (1 John 3:10)

Verse 10 summarizes a discussion that began all the way back in 2:3. It also prepares us for a more extended discussion to follow on the important subject of love. Two simple and fundamental tests are set forth in this text that distinguish a child of God from a child of the Devil. First, do you do what is right? Second, do you love others? John says it is that simple. In these verses, John has put the issue in negative terms (*not* doing what is right and *not* loving others). But they clearly are meant to be an exhortation to believers: "Show yourselves to be true children of God! Practice these two virtues!" Plummer is right in showing, however, that the two are actually interrelated: "Love is righteousness in relation to others" (Plummer, *The Epistles of St. John*, 128). Those who hate sin, who have been set free from the Devil, and who are born of God will do what is right and love others.

This is what our God does. This is what His children will do. You see, the child has the distinguishing marks of his parents. What he sees his Father do, that is what he will do. What he sees His Savior do, that is what he will do too. Sadly, if the Devil is your spiritual father, you will reveal your parentage by practicing sin and hating others (cf. John 8:44). I guess the question really is, "Who's your daddy?!" Your life will provide a clear and undeniable witness.

Conclusion

John has shown us that "the Son of God was revealed for this purpose: to destroy the Devil's works" (1 John 3:8). Desiderius Erasmus (1466–1536), a leading Christian humanist of the sixteenth century, got it right when in his *Paraphrase on Mark* he said, "By a carpenter mankind was made, and only by that Carpenter can mankind be remade." The carpenter from Nazareth, the Son of God, has indeed remade us—redeemed by His blood, regenerated by the Spirit, reconciled with the Father, and ready for service. What a joy it is to be a child of God! What a blessing to have been saved and set free from the shackles of sin and the tyranny of Satan! Jesus, thank You for coming.

Reflect and Discuss

1. Discuss Anyabwile's four different audiences from the beginning of this chapter (p. 65). What are some characteristics of each? How is it helpful to think about all four of these groups when preaching and teaching?
2. How does John define sin? How does a biblical understanding of sin help us understand the gospel rightly?
3. How does Christ's person (who He is) qualify Him to deal with sin?
4. Why do Christians still sin given verse 6?
5. How does Jesus' work destroy the Devil's work?
6. What is the connection between the Devil's work and personal holiness? How is sin contrary to Christ's work?
7. Why is external holiness a mark of regeneration if the new birth is a work in our hearts?
8. How are righteousness and love related? Are these virtues choices we make or natural results of holiness?

How's Your Love Life?
A Superlative Witness That You Belong to Jesus

1 JOHN 3:11-18

Main Idea: Those who truly belong to God in Christ will live and love after the pattern of Jesus rather than the pattern of the world.

I. **Love One Another and Do Not Follow the Example of Cain (3:11-15).**
   A. Love is at the heart of the gospel (3:11-13).
   B. Love provides assurance that we have eternal life (3:14-15).

II. **Serve One Another and Follow the Example of Jesus (3:16-18).**
   A. Service to others may mean dying (3:16).
   B. Service to others always involves giving (3:17-18).

One of the most effective ways of teaching is using contrasts and comparisons. For example, I might contrast what it means to be a *male* with what it means to be a *female*. I might highlight the attributes of a *tall person* by standing him next to a *short person*. Boy/girl. Big/small. Fast/slow. Up/down. North/South. East/West. Winner/loser. These are all simple examples, but we use this teaching technique all the time. And this technique is not new. The apostle John also found drawing comparisons and contrasts to be an effective means of teaching theology and spiritual truth. Throughout 1 John, the apostle draws our attention to various contrasts:

Walk in darkness/Walk in light	1:6-7
Say we have no sin/Confess our sins	1:8-9
Keep God's commands/Do not keep God's commands	2:3-5
Those who love the world/Those who love the Father	2:15
They/Us	2:19
Antichrist/Christ	2:22
Deny Christ/Confess Christ	2:23
Confident at Christ's coming/Ashamed at Christ's coming	2:28
Those who commit sin/Those who do what is right	3:4-7
Children of the Devil/Children of God	3:10
Hates his brother/Loves his brother	3:10ff

John will now develop this last theme of hate/love as he moves us into the second major section of this letter. In 1:5–3:10 the message was "God is Light." Now in 3:11–5:12 the message is "God is Love." And because God is love, Christians are to love one another.

The importance of Christians loving one another cannot be overstated. In fact, to hate your brother is akin to murdering your brother, just like Cain murdered Abel in Genesis 4. Jesus teaches us that loving one another provides a superlative witness to a watching world. Remember what He said in John 13:35: "By this all people will know that you are My disciples, if you have love for one another." Love is the quintessential evidence that says to others, "I belong to and follow after Jesus. My life is to be identified with His."

Once again, by vivid contrast, John instructs us and enables us to examine the genuineness of our love life. The test is convicting. It is also clear.

Love One Another and Do Not Follow the Example of Cain
1 JOHN 3:11-15

Verse 11 flows naturally out of verse 10. The child of God, having been born of God, does what is right, which includes loving his brother. In contrast, the child of the Devil does not do what is right, and he hates (even murders!) his brother. There is a crystal clear contrast between children of God and children of the Devil, between lovers and haters. To make this plain, John goes back in time, all the way back to the beginning. There, he draws our attention to the first murder in human history, the murder of Abel by his brother Cain. He will address both the act and the sinister source behind the act. Just as God delights in giving life, the Devil equally delights in producing death by instigating murder.

Love Is at the Heart of the Gospel (1 John 3:11-13)

In language reminiscent of 1 John 1:5, John says he has a message, a report, which his readers had heard at the beginning of their new life in Christ through the gospel. And what is the gospel message that they had received at conversion? It is simply this: "We should love [continually] one another" (v. 11). This word about love was not just something they heard at the beginning of their Christian experience. It is a word repeated again and again throughout the New Testament.

I give you a new command: Love one another. Just as I have loved you, you must also love one another. (John 13:34)

This is My command: Love one another as I have loved you. (John 15:12)

This is what I command you: Love one another. (John 15:17)

Show family affection to one another with brotherly love. (Rom 12:10)

Do not owe anyone anything, except to love one another, for the one who loves another has fulfilled the law. (Rom 13:8)

For you were called to be free, brothers; only don't use this freedom as an opportunity for the flesh, but serve one another through love. (Gal 5:13)

Therefore I, the prisoner for the Lord, urge you to walk worthy of the calling you have received, with all humility and gentleness, with patience, accepting one another in love. (Eph 4:1-2)

And may the Lord cause you to increase and overflow with love for one another and for everyone, just as we also do for you. (1 Thess 3:12)

About brotherly love: You don't need me to write you because you yourselves are taught by God to love one another. (1 Thess 4:9)

And let us be concerned about one another in order to promote love and good works. (Heb 10:24)

By obedience to the truth, having purified yourselves for sincere love of the brothers, love one another earnestly from a pure heart. (1 Pet 1:22)

Above all, maintain an intense love for each other, since love covers a multitude of sins. (1 Pet 4:8)

And in this letter of 1 John, we will see this command to love given again in 3:23 and 4:7,11,12. It also appears in 2 John 5. Obviously, God thinks our loving one another is extremely important.

John, following Jesus, says we are to love consistently and comprehensively, continually and individually. Play no favorites. Show no biases. Practice no discriminations among your brothers and sisters.

After all, we are family! Love for others flows out of God's love for us. It is at the heart of the gospel. To love our brothers and sisters is to stand in stark contrast to the first murderer in the Bible, the man named Cain. This tragic and well-known story, recorded in Genesis 4:1-6, is the only direct Old Testament reference in 1 John. Cain's actions revealed his true spiritual father, the Devil (cf. 1 John 3:10). As Jesus taught in John 8:44,

> You are of your father the Devil, and you want to carry out your father's desires. He was a murderer from the beginning and has not stood in the truth, because there is no truth in him. When he tells a lie, he speaks from his own nature, because he is a liar and the father of liars.

The word "murder" means to butcher, slay, or slaughter. It speaks of a violent and brutal killing. And what were Cain's motives? Moved by his spiritual father, "the evil one," his heart was filled with jealously, envy, and resentment. Abel brought a sacrifice to God that was acceptable and "righteous." Cain brought one that was evil and unacceptable (v. 12). Cain hated Abel over this and murdered his own flesh and blood.

To all of this John says, "Do not be surprised" (v. 13). It could be translated, "stop being surprised." It is natural for the world (represented by Cain) to hate you because its father hates you (cf. v. 1). Do not be surprised or caught off guard when people of this world, people like Cain, hate you. It is their nature. However, don't you be like Cain. Don't descend to their level. Resist that primal urge to return hate with hate, murder with murder. The gospel has changed you, and love is at the heart of the gospel message. Where the gospel has taken root, love will be the natural fruit.

Love Provides Assurance That We Have Eternal Life
(1 John 3:14-15)

Loving others has numerous positive benefits and blessings. One is that we know we have been born again and have eternal life. In fact, John says we have an abiding and settled knowledge "that we have passed from [spiritual] death to [eternal] life because we love [continually] our brothers." In contrast, "The one who does not love remains in death" (v. 14).

Now, let's be clear on what John is saying and what he is not saying. John *is* saying that continually loving others out of "gospel gratitude" (cf. v. 16) for all that Jesus has done is evidence, a proof, that we have definitely and decisively moved from the realm of spiritual death into the realm of spiritual life. What he *is not* saying is that eternal life is earned by loving others, but rather that loving others is evidence that we already have eternal life. It therefore becomes another avenue of assurance of eternal life. As I love my brothers and sisters in the community of faith well, I am assured that I am in the family of God.

Interestingly, the word for "brother" occurs 15 times in this letter and almost always has in view the family of God. John, no doubt, would affirm our love for all men and women in general, but here he calls for us to love our brothers and sisters in Christ in particular. Paul says something similar to this in Galatians 6:10 when he writes, "Therefore, as we have opportunity, we must work for the good of all, especially for those who belong to the household of faith."

Those whose lives are characterized by hatred give evidence that they have never been born again, that they "remain in death" (v. 14; cf. Eph 2:1-3). Further, not only do they live in the world of spiritual death; they are actually murderers in the eyes of God (v. 15). John is clear: an attitude of hate in your heart is equivalent to having murder in your heart. John again is drawing from words he had heard from Jesus. In the Sermon on the Mount, Jesus said in Matthew 5:21-22,

> You have heard that it was said to our ancestors, Do not murder, and whoever murders will be subject to judgment. But I tell you, everyone who is angry with his brother will be subject to judgment. And whoever says to his brother, "Fool!" will be subject to the Sanhedrin. But whoever says, "You moron!" will be subject to hellfire.

John says it is really quite simple: no love, no life. Love and hate are moral, spiritual opposites. Both cannot reside at the same time in the same heart. "Our love for one another is the flower and fruit that indicates eternal life is at the root" (Anyabwile, unpulished sermon notes).

Serve One Another and Follow the Example of Jesus
1 JOHN 3:16-18

Real love, God's love, is *shown* as well as *spoken*. It is tangible and not theoretical. You see in our fallen, broken world how we are so often confused and unsure as to what real love is. Sometimes we are simply wrong in our understanding. Yes, we think about love, talk about love, write about love, and sing (a lot!) about love. But do we really and truly know what love is?

No doubt love was truly expressed, given, and received by Adam and Eve in the Garden of Eden up to the time of the fall. Then everything went terribly wrong, and murder soon followed with Cain killing Abel. And it hasn't stopped yet; it has only escalated. We see this clearly as more details emerge about the horrible abortion holocaust in China. On March 14, 2013, the Chinese Health Ministry reported that 336 million abortions have taken place in that country since 1971 (Strode, "China"). Such statistics stagger us, but they should not surprise us. The god of this world (2 Cor 4:4) appears to be winning the day. And yet, in another amazing reversal, there will be the death of death through a death, the death of the Son of God who "laid down His life for us" (1 John 3:16).

Service to Others May Mean Dying (1 John 3:16)

Many have noticed the beautiful relationship that exists between John 3:16 and 1 John 3:16. The former is a demonstration of love. The latter is an explanation of love. John 3:16 says that God gave His Son for us. First John 3:16 says we should give ourselves for others. The Bible says that if you want to see love, look at the cross! The Bible says that if you want to show love, look at the cross! The Bible says that if you want to know love, look at the cross! The Bible says that if you want to live love, look at the cross!

We come to an acquired and abiding knowledge of what love is when we consider the penal, substitutionary sacrifice of the Son of God on our behalf. He lived the life we should have lived but didn't. And He died the death we should have died but now don't have to die. Love, at its core, is about self-sacrifice and self-substitution. And in our case, it is for those who are completely and totally unworthy. In the song "You Are My King," Chris Tomlin reminds us that our King died on our behalf! Once we take in and really get our head around this amazing truth, our only reasonable reaction is to honor God. If we really understand the magnitude of what has been done for us and the implications for eternity, we won't feel obligated to show gratitude; we won't be merely willing to be thankful; we will joyfully present our lives to God as a living sacrifice in grateful worship.

That is exactly what John tells us. Out of "gospel gratitude" for His laying down His life for us, "we ought to lay down our own lives for the brothers." Warren Wiersbe says, "'Self-preservation' is the first law of physical life, but 'self-sacrifice' is the first law of spiritual life" (*Be Real*, 127). Jesus said it like this in John 15:13: "No one has greater love than this, that someone would lay down his life for his friends."

Service to Others Always Involves Giving (1 John 3:17-18)

"I would die for you" sounds noble and spiritual. It sounds awesome. But while you are willing to die for me, would you give me something to eat? Could you share an extra shirt or better yet, a coat? Could you let me sleep on your couch until I get back on my feet? Could you help out with my electric bill or a few meds for my sick kids? You see, I don't need you to die for me. I just need a little help. "Talk is cheap" is a modern axiom, and I suspect that the concept originated in the Bible! In verses 17-18, John gets down where the rubber meets the road and provides some basic, real, and practical advice about love in the context of everyday living.

Verse 17 introduces a negative example using a "greater to lesser" argument based on verse 16. Jesus had a life to give and you have stuff ("this world's goods") to give. Jesus saw your need and gave His life. You, however, see your brother's need and "close your eyes" (lit. "entrails," i.e., feelings). How then, "can God's love reside in" you? The obvious and undeniable answer is, "It doesn't." It is not there.

John knows that our hearts control our hands. A closed heart will always result in closed hands and is evidence that your heart has never been opened by the "key of the gospel" of God's grace poured out in Jesus. The brother of Jesus, James, has the same concern as he writes in Jas 2:15-17,

> If a brother or sister is without clothes and lacks daily food and one
> of you says to them, "Go in peace, keep warm, and eat well," but you
> don't give them what the body needs, what good is it? In the same way
> faith, if it doesn't have works, is dead by itself.

Dead faith. Dead love. Neither one does any good to others.

John concludes his argument in verse 18 with a simple maxim that follows a negative-to-positive line of reasoning: "Little children, we must not love with word or speech, but with truth and action." Love is so much more than making a good profession or a great speech that uses impressive rhetoric (cf. 1 Cor 13:1-3). No, love is an action word that always expresses itself in good deeds done in the context of truth. John adds the word "truth" for a very good reason. Words can be empty and actions can be hypocritical. You may choose to do nothing, though your words promise much. On the other hand, you may do something for someone, but your motives are impure and your intentions evil. We call this manipulation. God cares about both our *motives* and our *actions*. He wants us to love and care for others just like we have been loved and cared for by Jesus. Once more, it is clear isn't it? Do you want to see love in deed and in truth? Just look to the cross.

Conclusion

Living out the gospel means having open ears, open eyes, and open hands for the hurting. It means loving others as we have been loved by Jesus. The late John Stott summarized it so well:

> Hatred characterizes the world, whose prototype is Cain.
> It originates in the Devil, issues in murder, and is evidence
> of spiritual death. Love characterizes the church, whose
> prototype is Christ. It originates in God, issues in self-sacrifice,
> and is evidence of eternal life. (*The Letters of John*, 148)

So, let us not just talk about love; let us truly demonstrate love. After all, Jesus didn't just *say* something. He *did* something!

Reflect and Discuss

1. Why is brotherly love important for Christians to express to one another? What are some important biblical passages on love?
2. How does John use Cain to exhort his readers to love? How is the world like Cain?
3. Why should we not be surprised that the world hates Christians? Does this mean that we never fight for justice?
4. How does our willingness to love reveal what is going on in our hearts? Why does John focus on love for other Christians?
5. In what sense are murder and hatred the same thing? How are they similar and different before God?
6. What is the difference between love as a sentiment and love that acts? Which is John's main concern here?

7. How does Jesus' example show us how to love?
8. Why do you think John is concerned with showing love through "this world's goods" rather than just with spiritual support, encouragement, etc.?
9. How far are you willing to go to show to others the love that Jesus showed you? How's your love life?

Gospel Truths That Will Heal a Hurting Heart and Cure a Condemning Conscience

1 JOHN 3:18-24

Main Idea: God uses biblical truths and the gift of His Spirit to provide assurance and comfort to His beloved children.

I. **Love for Others Reassures Our Hearts That We Belong to God (3:18-19).**
II. **God Is the Perfect Judge Who Sees Everything (3:20).**
III. **Be Confident That God Answers Our Prayers (3:21-22).**
IV. **Believe That Jesus Christ Is the Son of God, and Love One Another (3:23).**
V. **Abide in God and Know that God Abides in Us by the Gift of His Spirit (3:24).**

The human heart is a tender, vulnerable, and complex component of every single person. Who you are on the inside, what we sometimes call "the real you," is a gracious gift from God when it is functioning as our Creator intended. As an ethical barometer, it helps us to make moral choices. It also allows us to express emotions and feelings and to be self-reflective. Sometimes we like what we see when we look on the inside. At other times we are wounded and even crushed by what we find. Our inclination is to embrace platitudes like "trust your heart" and "let your conscience be your guide," but God tells us in Jeremiah 17:9, "The heart is more deceitful than anything else, and incurable—who can understand it?" Interestingly, the answer to this often quoted verse is found in the very next verse in Jeremiah: "I, Yahweh, examine the mind, I test the heart to give each according to his way."

From a pastoral perspective we should recognize there can be a number of reasons a person may have what John calls a condemning conscience or heart. James Boice notes,

> Self-condemnation can be due to a number of factors. It can be a matter of disposition; some people are just more introspective and melancholy than others. It may be a question of health; how a person feels inevitably affects how

he thinks. It may be due to specific sin. It may be due to
circumstances. But whatever the cause, the problem is a real
one and quite widespread. How is a believer to deal with such
doubt? (Boice, *The Epistles of John*, 121–22)

The apostle John recognized that those who have believed in Jesus
(3:23) could still suffer from a hurting heart, a condemning conscience.
He also knew there were some basic truths, all grounded in the good
news of the gospel, that could provide healing, the exact cure that is
needed. Some basic knowledge of what God has done and is doing in
the lives of those who have trusted in Jesus provides the precise remedy
for this all-too-common heart condition. The medicine is strong, but
the outcome for the patient is more than worth it.

Love for Others Reassures Our Hearts That We Belong to God
1 JOHN 3:18-19

John uses verse 18 as a "hinge verse" to connect two related passages
that have a common subject. The subject is love. When we love "with
truth and action" (v. 18), this reassures our hearts before God that we
are of the truth (v. 19). Assurance will spring forth in the heart, in the
conscience, when we demonstrate genuine and authentic love for others. It assures us that we are children of God. We have confidence in His
presence that He is our God and we are His children.

Loving others as God in Christ has loved us strengthens our hearts
and gives us assurance. Indeed by loving others in truth (v. 18) we come
to "know we belong to the truth" (v. 19). However, we must be honest.
Loving others is not always easy. Clearly it is easier said than done. After
all, at the heart of love is serving others as we have been served by Jesus.
Sometimes this service is public, noble, and newsworthy. Sometimes it
is private, humiliating, and unnoticed. It can be a challenge. Richard
Foster nails it when he writes in *Celebration of Discipline*,

> In some ways we would prefer to hear Jesus' call to deny father
> and mother, houses and land for the sake of the gospel than his
> word to wash feet. Radical self-denial gives the feel of adventure.
> . . . But in service we much experience the many little deaths of
> going beyond ourselves. Service banishes us to the mundane,
> the ordinary, the trivial. (*Celebration of Discipline*, 110)

Yes, love requires service. Service involves humility. And loving others in humble service gives us assurance that we belong to Jesus. That sounds like a life worth living, a path worth pursuing. And don't miss this: it is by this knowledge and truth in our minds that assurance is planted and flourishes in our hearts.

God Is the Perfect Judge Who Sees Everything
1 JOHN 3:20

Verse 20 can be a tricky and difficult verse to interpret, at least when it comes to the details. However, its basic meaning is clear. Even though Christ has propitiated all our sins by His perfect atoning work, we may experience a condemning heart or guilty conscience, something the great and omnipotent God does not want us to have. So when my conscience sends me on a guilt trip, I look in faith to the God who is greater than my vacillating heart and who assures me of my total and complete forgiveness through the perfect work of Jesus. I claim once more the wonderful truth of 1 John 1:9. John, therefore, addresses directly this guilty conscience and the way to deal with it. In 3:20 he does so in the context of the omniscience of God, and in verses 21-22 he will do so in the context of prayer.

We know that the Bible teaches that it is possible to be saved and yet have doubts and become discouraged. In such instances, we would be wise to take the threefold test we have already seen in 1 John:

- **Belief**: Do I really believe rightly about Jesus?
- **Obedience**: Am I really obeying God as I ought?
- **Love**: Is my love for others what it should be?

Sometimes I doubt; sometimes I disobey; sometimes hate comes, seemingly out of nowhere, and these things bother me. That is bad, right? No, it is actually good. Those who do not know Christ ask none of these questions! Such issues do not bother those with hard hearts. But they can trouble the Christian.

When your heart hurts and your conscience condemns you, look to God. Look to Christ and the gospel because He "is greater than our conscience, and He knows all things." Now, exactly how does God apply the healing balm of His Word in such situations? I believe He does so in several ways.

When we do not love in action and truth (v. 18), God—who is
(1) greater than our hearts and (2) knows all things—deals with us.
Sometimes our heart rightly condemns us, blames us, and judges us for
not loving others in a real, true, and genuine sense. Our conscience
calls us out! God in grace and mercy can help us overcome and conquer
this. He will motivate us (v. 17) to just say no to a hard and unloving
heart. He sees everything, so He knows what is going on. Indeed, He
knows our hearts better than we know them ourselves. He will inspire
us, encourage us, and challenge us to love others just like He has loved
us (v. 16).

Our conscience can be too lenient in its verdict. However, our
conscience may also be too severe, forgetting that "no condemnation
now exists for those in Christ Jesus" (Rom 8:1). God is greater than
all, and He knows all. He is the perfect judge. None of the believer's
failures or successes escape His notice. This is the difference between
conscience and omniscience! He knows! He sees! Yet he still accepts us
in Christ!

Remembering who we are in Christ will provide assurance as we
stand before the perfect Judge, who also happens to be our Father. So
be honest. Tell God, "I don't know myself, sometimes, why I do what I do
(or don't do). But You do know me perfectly, so I commit all judgment to
You! I put it all in Your hands." Pray Psalm 139:23, where the Bible says,
"Search me, God, and know my heart; test me and know my concerns."
Trust what Paul says in 1 Corinthians 4:3-5:

> It is of little importance to me that I should be evaluated by you or by
> any human court. In fact, I don't even evaluate myself. For I am not
> conscious of anything against myself, but I am not justified by this.
> The One who evaluates me is the Lord. Therefore don't judge anything
> prematurely, before the Lord comes, who will both bring to light what is
> hidden in darkness and reveal the intentions of the hearts. And then
> praise will come to each one from God.

Be Confident That God Answers Our Prayers
1 JOHN 3:21-22

There is a beautiful and natural flow to John's argument in these verses.
Loving others as we have been loved by Jesus assures us that we are in
the truth, even when we don't love perfectly. God says, "Trust Me, not

your conscience, which is not infallible and is not always correct." Now that we are confident before God (v. 20), we can be confident when we pray (vv. 21-22). John again addresses his readers as "Dear friends" (Gk *agapetoi*, cf. 4:1,7), showing concern and compassion for those struggling with a hurting heart and a condemning conscience. It is followed by words of encouragement.

The sense of what John says is this: When we trust the judgment of our conscience to our great God, who is omniscient about everything, our confidence shifts from being based on our experience and our feelings to being based on God's Word and what He says about us. He tells me there is no condemnation for those who are in Christ Jesus (Rom 8:1,31-34). Seeing who I am in Christ, I have confidence and boldness, "the boldness with which the son appears before the Father, and not that which the accused appears before the Judge" (Westcott, *The Epistles of St. John*, 118).

This confidence before God, resulting from a clear conscience in Christ, provides motivation and assurance as I approach Father God in prayer: "If our conscience doesn't condemn us, we have confidence before God and can receive whatever we ask from Him because we keep His commands and do what is pleasing in His sight" (vv. 21-22). My request made in prayer flows from a heart and life that, first, delights in keeping His commands and, second, does what pleases Him. These provide the crucial theological context for the later promise in 1 John: "Whenever we ask anything according to His will, He hears us. And if we know that He hears whatever we ask, we know that we have what we have asked Him for" (5:14-15).

The wonderful Baptist preacher Charles Spurgeon had words of wisdom that drive home the truths of these verses:

> "If our heart condemn us not, then have we confidence toward God; and whatsoever we ask, we receive of him." He who has a clear conscience comes to God with confidence, and that confidence of faith ensures to him the answer of his prayer. Childlike confidence makes us pray as none else can. It makes a man pray for great things, which he would never have asked for if he had not learned this confidence; and makes him pray for little things which a great many are afraid to ask for, because they have not yet felt towards God the confidence of children. . . .

The man of *obedience* is the man whom God will hear, because his obedient heart leads him to pray humbly, and with submission, for he feels it to be his highest desire that the Lord's will should be done. Hence it is that the man or obedient heart prays like an oracle; his prayers are prophecies. Is he not one with God? Doth he not desire and ask for exactly what God intends? How can a prayer shot from such a bow ever fail to reach its target? (Spurgeon, "The Conditions of Power in Prayer," emphasis added)

Believers with clear consciences, confident access, and obedient lives that please Christ can be assured that God will hear and answer their prayers for their good and for His glory. After all, I am a trusting child coming to a loving Father who knows all my sins and imperfections and still loves me and accepts me anyway in His Son.

Believe That Jesus Is the Son of God, and Love One Another
1 JOHN 3:23

This verse (together with the one that follows) is quietly but clearly Trinitarian, and it provides a grand and glorious summary of the Bible. It is interesting how John packages this verse. Fundamentally, there is one comprehensive command expressed in two parts. First, there must be an explicit belief in the Son, Jesus Christ. This is John's doctrinal test. Second, there must be an active love for one another. This is John's moral test.

God's command is "that we believe in the name of His Son Jesus Christ." Every word in this command is significant. This is the first of nine occurrences of the word *"believe"* in 1 John (cf. also 3:23; 4:1,16; 5:1,5,10[3x],13). It means, "to trust or rely on." Jesus' "name" conveys His person and work and all that He is and accomplishes. That Jesus is the "Son" emphasizes His eternal deity and unique relationship to the Father. "Jesus" is His human name, equivalent to the Hebrew name Joshua. It means "Yahweh saves" or "Yahweh is salvation." And "Christ" means "Anointed One," the Messiah of God.

Let's put it all together. To believe in the name of God's Son Jesus Christ is to place your trust, your faith, in Him and only Him and all that He is—the divine Son, the incarnate Deity, the sinless human, the perfect atonement for our sin, the Messianic Savior. You trust all of Him, not some, part, or even most. You trust the biblical Christ or you trust in no Christ at all.

We also "love one another as He commanded us." This command appears repeatedly throughout the Bible. Arguably, the most significant appearance of the command is found in John 13:34-35, where Jesus said on the night He was betrayed,

> *I give you a new command: Love one another. Just as I have loved you, you must also love one another. By this all people will know that you are My disciples, if you have love for one another.*

It appears again in John's Gospel in 15:12 and 17.

Warren Wiersbe nails the essence of this verse quite well for us: "Faith toward God and love toward man sum up a Christian's obligations. Christianity is 'faith which worketh by love' (Gal 5:6)" (*Be Real*, 133–34). John Piper helpfully adds,

> The one all-embracing commandment of this letter is that we believe and that we love. These are the foundations of our assurance because these are the evidence of God's work; they are the testimony of his Spirit. ("Test the Spirits")

This last statement provides a natural transition to our final observation.

Abide in God and Know That God Abides in Us by the Gift of His Spirit
1 JOHN 3:24

John addresses our keeping the commands of God for the fourth time in verses 22-24, but now he adds a blessing that flows from our obedience. Working backwards and paraphrasing the verse helps us clarify what John is teaching us. By the Holy Spirit, whom God has given us as a grace gift, we know that God abides in us and we abide in God. And, as a habit of his new life in Christ, the one who abides in God continually keeps His commands. John's point is that keeping God's commands and abiding in God always go together. Having the Spirit of God and abiding or remaining in God always go together. John's emphasis on *abiding* is clear in that 54 of the 102 New Testament occurrences of this word (Gk *meno*) appear in John's writings.

John clearly wants us to understand that the Spirit—the true Spirit who stands in radical contrast to the false spirits of antichrist (cf. 4:1-6)—comes as a gift, not as something God was obliged to give us. He is given to us as a grace gift; He is not something we can earn or merit. In saying the Spirit has already been given to us, John looks to the past, to our conversion, the moment in time when we first believed the gospel. That is when we received the Spirit. Verse 24 is the first direct mention of the Holy Spirit in 1 John. This Third Person of the triune God is essential to God's abiding in us and our abiding in God. He is crucial to helping us discern the false spirits— the spirits of error—that do not confess that Jesus is from God (cf. 4:3). John Stott explains the Spirit's role in our abiding in this way:

> The Spirit, whose presence is the test of Christ's living in us, manifests himself objectively in our life and conduct. It is he who inspires us to confess Jesus as the Christ come in the flesh, as John immediately proceeds to show (4:1ff; cf. 2:20,27). It is also he who empowers us to live righteously and to love our brothers and sisters (cf. 4:13; Gal 5:16,22). So if we would set our hearts at rest, when they accuse and condemn us, we must look for evidence of the Spirit's working, and particularly whether he is enabling us to believe in Christ, to obey God's commands and to love our brothers; for the condition of Christ dwelling in us and of our dwelling in him is this comprehensive obedience (24a), and the evidence of the indwelling is the gift of the Spirit (24b). (*The Letters of John*, 154–55)

Conclusion

A number of years ago I met a 55-year-old man who asked if he could share his conversion testimony. I said, "Sure! I would love to hear it." He told me he had trusted Christ at the age of 50, just 5 years before. He went on to say he was a recovering alcoholic and drug addict who had experienced several failed marriages, all of which were his fault. He said he blamed no one, that he had made bad choices and dumb decisions throughout most of his life. Then, with tears streaming down his face, he began to talk about his childhood and a dad who criticized and condemned him at every turn. He said, "You know, all I can remember about my childhood was my daddy saying things like, 'Boy you can't do anything right. Boy, you're just downright dumb. Boy, you will never grow up to amount to anything.'" He then added, "I guess I grew up to be exactly what my daddy said I would be."

But then, with a gentle smile and a twinkle in his eye, he quietly and humbly whispered, "But 5 years ago, when I met Jesus, I got a new daddy. And this daddy loves me. He believes in me. He thinks I can do anything!"

In Christ, we do get a new daddy, a perfect daddy, a perfect heavenly Father. This Father longs for you to have a healthy heart and a clear conscience. And you can! Recall who you are in Him through Christ and by the Spirit. Love others as you have been loved by Him. Obey His commands and please Him out of "gospel gratitude" for who He is and what He has done. These are truths with the power to save. These are truths with the power to heal.

Reflect and Discuss

1. What are some reasons that believers might have a hurting heart? A condemning conscience?

2. Why should love for others give us assurance of salvation? Isn't love a natural feeling?

3. How can doubt and guilt actually serve to assure us of God's presence in our lives? Do you know anyone who never has doubts and never feels guilt? Does that seem healthy?

4. Why do we look to God for assurance and not to our own consciences? What aspect of our conscience is untrustworthy?

5. Why can we be sure that God will answer our prayers? Does this give license to ask for whatever we want?

6. Why must we keep John's doctrinal test and his moral test together? What happens if we relax on one or the other?

7. Why is the Holy Spirit such an astounding gift to every Christian? How does His presence provide assurance? How does His presence enable obedience?

Test the Spirits! They Are Not All from God!

1 JOHN 4:1-6

Main Idea: Genuine Christians will avoid false teachers and will recognize that true teachers possess the Spirit of God and preach Jesus Christ as the risen Lord.

I. Are You Following False Prophets (4:1)?
II. Are You Confessing the True Jesus (4:2-3)?
III. Are You Trusting in the Greater Spirit (4:4)?
IV. Are You Listening to the Right Teachers (4:5-6)?

In 2013, Christian rapper Shai Linne stirred quite a controversy with his song "Fal$e Teacher$." It is a critique of the prosperity gospel, and in it he does the unacceptable in our hypertolerant/noncritical day: he names names. In the song, Shai particularly calls on Christians outside of America not to be deceived by these "wolves in sheep's clothing" (Matt 7:15) who export their heresies around the world. He says,

Don't be deceived by this funny biz,
if you come to Jesus for money, then he's not your God,
      money is!
Jesus is not a means to an end, the Gospel is.

He came to redeem us from sin, and that is the message
      forever I yell!
If you're living your best life now you're heading for hell!

Turn off TBN, that channel is overrated.
The pastors speak bogus statements, financially motivated.

It's kind of like a pyramid scheme.
Visualize heretics Christianizing the American dream.

It's foul and deceitful, they're lying to people,
      teaching that camels squeeze through the eye of a needle!

John Piper via Twitter said of the song, "My, my, Shai, this is good."

Calling out and identifying false teachers is neither fun nor popular. It is, however, both biblical and necessary. They are often more dangerous and more plentiful than many Christians realize. The apostle John makes that clear in 1 John 4:1-6. In words similar to those he penned earlier in 2:18-27, the last living apostle draws a contrast between true prophets and false prophets, the true Christ and antichrists, and that which is of the Spirit of God and that which is of the spirits of this world. Six times he will use the phrase "from God" and six times he will use the phrase "the world." Amazingly, those who are of "the world" and not "from God" have worked their way into the churches. Again we are reminded that our greatest dangers are not from without but from within. Therefore we must "test the spirits" (v. 1) because they are not all from God. John provides a fourfold test we must take. This exam is more important than any you will ever take in any school. Its results are of eternal significance.

Are You Following False Prophets?
1 JOHN 4:1

John again begins with a word of affection and love: "Dear friends" (Gk *agapetoi*). He deeply cares for these brothers and sisters in Christ and he is very much aware that danger is lurking about, possibly within. John wants them to be aware of the fact that not every spiritual teacher is a credible teacher. There are spiritual deceivers and liars out there, and they work hard to earn our trust, our allegiance. So John says, "Do not believe every spirit, but test the spirits to determine if they are from God." Both "believe" and "test" are imperatives calling for continuous action and vigilance. Further, the word "test" carries the idea of putting something to rigorous examination to discover its genuineness. And "do not believe" and "test" are in the plural. This is a churchwide community responsibility. We are *all* to be doctrine detectives, theological investigators!

Our goal is to determine if these prophets are from God or if their origin is to be found in another source, in a different kind of spirit. John's point is straightforward: Behind every prophet, every proclamation, there is an energizing spirit. Their message will inform us as to the origin and source of their message. They are not all from God. Watch! Listen! Test! Here a healthy dose of "spiritual skepticism" is warranted. In fact, it is essential for the health and well-being of the Christian community. And note, these false prophets (Gk *pseudoprophetai*) are everywhere: "many . . . have gone out into the world." They are demonically inspired missionaries on satanic assignment. They are not simply guilty of theological error; they are guilty of theological heresy! False prophets are not new to John's readers. They have been around for a very long time.

If a prophet or someone who has dreams arises among you and proclaims a sign or wonder to you, and that sign or wonder he has promised you comes about, but he says, "Let us follow other gods," which you have not known, "and let us worship them," do not listen to that prophet's words or to that dreamer. For the LORD your God is testing you to know whether you love the LORD your God with all your heart and all your soul. You must follow the LORD your God and fear Him. You must keep His commands and listen to His voice; you must worship Him and remain faithful to Him. That prophet or dreamer must be put to death, because he has urged rebellion against the LORD your God who brought you out of the land of Egypt and redeemed you from the place of slavery, to turn you from the way the LORD your God has commanded you to walk. You must purge the evil from you. (Deut 13:1-5)

"But the prophet who dares to speak a message in My name that I have not commanded him to speak, or who speaks in the name of other gods—that prophet must die." You may say to yourself, "How can we recognize a message the LORD has not spoken?" When a prophet speaks in the LORD's name, and the message does not come true or is not fulfilled, that is a message the LORD has not spoken. The prophet has spoken it presumptuously. Do not be afraid of him. (Deut 18:20-22)

I wish you would put up with a little foolishness from me. Yes, do put up with me. For I am jealous over you with a godly jealousy, because I have promised you in marriage to one husband—to present a pure virgin to Christ. But I fear that, as the serpent deceived Eve by his cunning, your minds may be seduced from a complete and pure devotion to Christ. For if a person comes and preaches another Jesus, whom we did not preach, or you receive a different spirit, which you had not received, or a different gospel, which you had not accepted, you put up with it splendidly. (2 Cor 11:1-4)

There is a tendency with most people to ascribe any unusual phenomenon to God. Such a lack of discernment opens the door for false teaching and provides an opportunity for demonic activity to invade the church. Remember: spiritual or religious activity is not necessarily godly activity! Watch and wait. Look and listen. Evaluate the message and the messenger by the Word of God. False prophets are deceptive in their message. And they have their own Great Commission, having been sent out "into the world."

You cannot say, "I was never warned." Jesus warned us (Matt 7:15; 24:11,14; Mark 13:21-23). Paul warned us (Acts 20:28-30). Peter warned us (2 Pet 2:1-22). Jude warned us (Jude 4-19). Where there is truth, error will be lurking in the background. Be on the lookout.

Are You Confessing the True Jesus?
1 JOHN 4:2-3

In *The Gospel in a Pluralist Society*, Lesslie Newbigin writes,

> The gospel is news of what has happened. The problem of communicating it in a pluralist society is that it simply disappears into the undifferentiated ocean of information. It represents one opinion among millions of others. It cannot be "the truth," since in a pluralist society truth is not one but many. It may be "true for you," but it cannot be true for everyone. To claim that it is true for everyone is simply arrogance. It is permitted as one opinion among many. (*The Gospel in a Pluralist Society*, 242)

Once again John makes it plain that Christianity is rooted and grounded in "the Christological question": What do you believe about Jesus? If He is just another enlightened religious teacher, He is permitted and tolerated as one opinion, one option, among many. If, however, He is the very incarnation of God, then the gospel and only the gospel is true and He is the only viable option for salvation amid the multitude of imposters.

Testing the spirits of verse 1 is greatly aided by asking "the Jesus question" of verses 2 and 3. "This is how you know," recognize, come to understand, "the Spirit of God" and those who bear His gospel message. Verse 2 puts the issue in a positive light and verse 3 in the negative. What confession bears witness to the presence of the Spirit of God? It is this: "Jesus Christ [the Messiah of God] has come [perf. tense] in the flesh [He is the incarnation of God]." Such a confession is not mere words or some glib statement. It is heartfelt, mind-engaged, and soul-committed. It is on this truth that authentic Christianity stands or falls—that there was a true, genuine, and permanent wedding of deity and humanity in the person of Jesus Christ, God's only Son.

The Spirit of God always honors Jesus Christ, the Son of God. Jesus said in John 16:14 concerning the Spirit, "He will glorify Me, because He will take from what is Mine and declare it to you." If there is no glorifying of Jesus as God incarnate then there is no Spirit of God present. Amazingly, even demons got it right and recognized the deity of Jesus while He walked on earth, though they certainly did not worship Him for it (Mark 1:24; 3:4; 5:7-8). Tragically, demons have a better theology than do some professing Christians, pastors, teachers, and theologians.

Verse 3 is the antithesis of verse 2. Those who deny the truth of the incarnation of the Son of God (1) are not of God and (2) are of the antichrist. When it comes to what people believe about Jesus, the early church was plagued much like the twenty-first century. Already there were people who refused to believe the truth about God sending His Son as the Savior of the world in the person of Jesus. *Docetists* said Jesus was a phantom or ghostly spirit who only appeared to be human. A man named *Cerinthus* said the Spirit of God's Christ empowered the human Jesus at His baptism but left Him at the crucifixion. The bottom line is that they denied the genuine reality of the incarnation and the wedding of deity and humanity in the person of Jesus (see description of Docetists and Cerinthus on p. 6).

"Antichrist" here means "against Christ" (cf. 2:18,22; 2 John 7). John says you heard he was coming (and he is), and he (through his devilish spirits) is now already in the world. He was active in John's day, he is active in our day, and he will remain active until the day that Jesus comes again.

I. Howard Marshall well says, "If a person claims to believe in Jesus, it is proper to ask, 'Is your Jesus the real Jesus?'" (*The Epistles of John*, 207). What one thinks about Jesus has enormous consequences. In a real sense, it determines everything! Tell me what you think about Jesus, and I will tell you 95 percent of the rest of your theology. He is the center, the hub of all theology. All of it radiates out from Him. So once more: Are you confessing the true Christ? Do you confess with the apostles, "You are the Messiah, the Son of the living God" (Matt 16:16)?

Are You Trusting in the Greater Spirit?

1 JOHN 4:4

There is what we could call "a divine irony" for those who believe in and follow after Jesus. The opposition of Satan—the world system that daily assaults us, false teachers that seek to seduce us, faulty worldviews that attempt to confuse us, and our own sinfulness that yearns to enslave us—is divinely ordained to fail. Why? Because of the glorious truth of verse 4: "The One who is in you is greater than the one who is in the world." We have a Champion, a Victor, a source of power that all of these enemies from hell cannot overcome.

Again, John uses a word of tenderness: "little children." Interestingly, the phrase "You are from God" precedes this warm affirmation. It is fronted for emphasis and to add intensity: "You, yourselves, and no one else, are of God, little children. And you have conquered them (the world, the false prophets, those who are of the spirit of antichrist) in an abiding and settled fashion." How did we obtain this victory? The Greater Spirit, the Holy Spirit, is in you, and He is greater than he who is in the world. Is the world strong? Yes, but our God is infinitely stronger! Are false prophets wise? Yes, but our God is infinitely wiser! Is Satan great? Yes, but our God is infinitely greater! And this One who is infinitely stronger, wiser, and greater now and forever "is in you"!

By a true and faithful confession of Jesus as Messiah, I declare that I am God's. In response, God gives Himself to me through His Spirit and takes up residence in me and in each and every one who sincerely calls Jesus "Lord." Amazingly, the God who can live anywhere desires to live inside of you and me! I now move forward in a life of loving, sacrificial service, just as my suffering-servant Savior did (note what follows in 4:7-21). I can live confidently, blessed with supernaturally given assurance that I am His and that I fight a battle in which victory is mine for the taking. John Piper applies this truth beautifully in a twofold manner:

> 1. Do not take credit for your listening ear or your confessing heart or your correct view of Christ. Give credit to the Spirit who is in you, and give God the glory.
> 2. When you are threatened by any deception of the evil one—any temptation, or discouragement, or anxiety, or cowardice—remind yourself that "he who is in you is greater than he that is in the world." Almighty God abides within you. Trust him. For this is the victory that overcomes the world,

your faith (5:4) in the sovereign indwelling power of the Holy Spirit. ("Test the Spirits")

Are You Listening to the Right Teachers?

1 JOHN 4:5-6

John brings this section to a close with words that are simple and, at first blush, can sound rather arrogant. However, a closer look will reveal he is directing us to the exact place we should go and the teachers to whom we should listen. John draws a contrast between those of the world—the evil, organized system controlled by Satan (v. 5)—and those who are from God (v. 6). Those who are from the Devil's domain speak out of that worldview and with that spirit's inspiration. They speak satanic sermons. They deliver demonic discourses, and those who belong to that worldview listen to and embrace their teachings. Therefore, we should never be surprised when the lost think like lost people and live like lost people. This is true even for those who once claimed to believe in and follow Christ. Those enslaved to the world cannot help but listen to those who speak their own language.

Verse 6 paints a different picture. Those who know God through confessing Jesus as the incarnate Christ and Savior (cf. 4:10) listen to those who were with Him, who were commissioned by Him. They stay with the apostles and the prophets (cf. Eph 2:20) and refuse to move away from this true and trustworthy source even one inch! In John 8:47 Jesus says, "The one who is from God listens to God's words." This is a helpful commentary on the meaning of this verse. There is no "Jesus-plus" or "Bible-plus" theology for those who truly know God. And there is no "Jesus-minus" or "Bible-minus" theology either. This is how you can without question tell the difference between "the Spirit of truth and the spirit of deception."

Now that raises a very important and very practical question: How can we listen to the apostles when they have been dead for almost 2,000 years? I love the answer of Thabiti Anyabwile:

> Through a certain kind of preaching. The preaching that takes the apostles' words, explains their words, and applies their words is the kind of preaching that enables us to listen to them today. We call this expositional preaching because it exposes what the apostles have written and the meaning and

application of their words. When you listen to the word of
God expositionally preached, you are listening to the apostles,
and ultimately you are listening to God himself. (unpublished
sermon notes)

The phrase "spirit of deception" is interesting. It has the idea of
wandering away from the truth. False prophets and those who listen to
their teachings hang around the truth for a while, but they don't stay.
They wander away. Again and again, their error comes back to what
they think and believe about Jesus. The Bible says He is God, but they
wander away and deny His eternal deity. The Bible says He is sinless,
but they wander away and say He sinned or at least committed error.
The Bible says He did miracles, but they wander away and say these are
myths and fables. The Bible says He is the *only* Savior, but they wander
away and say He is only *a* savior. The Bible says He died on the cross for
our sins, but they wander away and deny penal substitution, calling it
cosmic child abuse. The Bible says He rose bodily from the dead, but
they wander away and say the disciples imagined that He did. The Bible
says He ascended into heaven as Lord, but they wander away and say this
is just another myth. The Bible says He is coming again, but they wander
away and say it's pop-Christian fiction. And finally, the Bible says He will
judge us all, but they wander away and say God is love and eventually all
will be saved. In the end, they say, "Love Wins."[2]

Conclusion
The sixteenth-century Reformer Martin Luther said it well:

It does no good to say: I will gladly confess Christ and His
Word in all articles except one or two which my tyrannical
masters will not tolerate. . . . But he who denies Christ in one
article or word has in this one article denied the same Christ
who would be denied in all articles; for there is but one Christ
in all His words, collectively and individually. (Luther, *What
Luther Says*, vol. 1, 407)

A battle is indeed raging for the hearts, the minds, and the souls
of men and women. Be a good soldier of Christ and the cross, of that

---

[2] See Rob Bell's heterodox book by this title.

which is true and that which is right. Test the spirits, confess Christ as Lord, trust the Holy Spirit who is within, and stay latched to the Word. Here is your strength. Here is your safety. Here is your salvation.

Reflect and Discuss

1. What is meant by "the world" in this passage? How can Christians effectively engage the world without surrendering their convictions?
2. Why do you think false prophets are still a problem in the church? How can we properly identify them?
3. Discuss the significance of the statement, "Spiritual or religious activity is not necessarily godly activity." How are they similar? How are they different?
4. Why is the question "Who is Jesus?" at the heart of orthodox Christianity? How does this question help us wade through religion in a pluralistic society?
5. What is meant by "the real Jesus"? How can we identify false ideas of Jesus? What are some that are prevalent today in the world? In the church?
6. In what way is the Spirit inside the Christian greater than the spirit who is in the world? How can it be true that Christians have already conquered evil spirits?
7. What are some examples of a "Jesus-plus" or a "Bible-plus" theology that characterizes false teaching? How can we slide into these ways of thinking?
8. When is it appropriate to call out false teachers? How can pastors be diligent to protect the flock without spending all their time calling out other people?

God Is Love

1 JOHN 4:7-12

Main Idea: The Father of Jesus is the God of Love, whose love is manifested in the sending of Christ and is perfected in the love displayed among His people.

I. **Love Has Its Origin in God (4:7-8).**
   A. Loving others gives evidence we have been born of God (4:7).
   B. Loving others gives evidence we know God (4:7-8).
II. **Love Is Seen in the Atoning Death of Jesus (4:9-10).**
   A. God sent His Son that we might live (4:9).
   B. God sent His Son that He might die (4:10).
III. **Love Is Perfected in Us When We Love Others (4:11-12).**
   A. God's love for us inspires us to love others (4:11).
   B. Our love for others brings His love to perfection (4:12).

Love, it has been said, has many faces. People see it in all sorts of shapes and sizes. I think it is interesting to note that sometimes we see it more clearly, not through the eyes of adults, but through the eyes of children. A group of professionals posed the following question to a group of four- to eight-year-olds: "What does love mean?" The answers they got, as one researcher said, "were broader and deeper than anyone could have imagined."

> "Love is when you go out to eat and give somebody most of your French fries without making them give you any of theirs." Chrissy—age 6
>
> "Love is what makes you smile when you're tired." Terri—age 4
>
> "Love is when my mommy makes coffee for my daddy and she takes a sip before giving it to him, to make sure the taste is OK." Danny—age 7
>
> "Love is what's in the room with you at Christmas if you stop opening presents and listen." Bobby—age 5
>
> "Love is when you tell a guy you like his shirt, then he wears it every day." Noelle—age 7
>
> "Love is when your puppy licks your face even after you left him alone all day." May Ann—age 4

"When you love somebody, your eyelashes go up and down and little
stars come out of you." Karen—age 7
"You really shouldn't say 'I love you' unless you mean it. But if you
mean it, you should say it a lot. People forget." Jessica—age 7
"When my grandmother got arthritis, she couldn't bend over and
paint her toenails anymore. So my grandfather does it for her
all the time, even when his hands got arthritis too. That's love."
Rebecca—age 8 (Sollee, "Love")

Well, it is one thing to get a child's perspective on love, but it is even
better to get God's perspective. Several times in the Bible God gives us
His thoughts on love. We find it in Song of Songs 8:5-14, 1 Corinthians
13, and here in 1 John 4:7-21. John has addressed the subject of love
already in 2:7-11 as an indication that one is walking in the light and in
3:11-24 as evidence that one is a child of God. Yet it is here, in 4:7-21,
that he provides his fullest treatment. As he calls us aside to talk about
this subject that some say "makes the world go 'round," John will take
us to the very origin and source of love: God Himself. In fact, love is
His very nature, and acting in love is His essential character. How do we
know? The cross! The cross of Golgotha is an everlasting monument to
the truth that our God is love.

Love Has Its Origin in God
1 JOHN 4:7-8

The word love (Gk *agape*) dominates 1 John 4:7–5:3. It appears over 30
times. Some have even said John is the expert on the subject. Paul is the
apostle of faith. Peter is the apostle of hope. James is the apostle of good
works. And John is the apostle of love.

There is little doubt we need an expert on love. In our culture love
is too often understood in selfish and sexual terms. The Word of God
paints a completely different picture. Here the words "sacrificial" and
"supernatural" jump out at us. Ultimately love comes from God and
is seen most clearly in the death of Jesus on the cross as He takes on
Himself the sins of the world.

Now we need to be clear. We are not saying lost people, non-
Christians, cannot love. Sadly, they sometimes love better than some
Christians do. This should not surprise us. Never forget that all persons
are made in the image of God. All persons, in spite of their depravity
and sinfulness, will give reflections of the One whose image they bear.

Further, God's grace and goodness is shared, in some measure, with the whole of His Creation. However, I believe that I. Howard Marshall is correct when he says, "Human love, however noble and however highly motivated, falls short if it refuses to include the Father and Son as the supreme objects of its affections" (*The Epistles of John*, 212). Such love unfortunately fails to honor the greatest love command of all, the command to love God with all that you are (Matt 22:36-38).

Loving Others Gives Evidence We Have Been Born of God (1 John 4:7)

With tender affection once again, John simply says to his spiritual children, "Love one another," a statement he will repeat twice more in this passage (vv. 11,12). Sam Storms says, "It occurs as an exhortation in 4:7, a statement of duty in 4:11, and as a hypothesis in 4:12" ("First John 4:7-21").

Why are we to "love one another"? The first reason John gives is this: "because love is from God." Real love, true love, always has its source in God. And whoever loves with a "God kind of love" gives evidence that they have been born of God. Regeneration, the new birth, being born again, unites spiritually dead, selfish hearts with God's living, loving heart so that His life becomes our life and His love our love (Piper, "The New Birth Produces Love"). John Piper puts it well:

> Love is from God the way heat is from fire, or the way light is from the sun. Love belongs to God's nature. It's woven into what he is. It's part of what it means to be God. The sun gives light because it is light. And fire gives heat because it is heat. So John's point is that in the new birth, this aspect of the divine nature becomes part of who you are. The new birth is the imparting to you of divine life, and an indispensable part of that life is love. God's nature is love, and in the new birth that nature becomes part of who you are. . . . When you are born again, God himself is imparted to you. He dwells in you and sheds abroad in your heart his love. And his aim is that this love be perfected in you. Notice the phrase "his love" in verse 12. The love that you have as a born again person is no mere imitation of the divine love. It is an experience of the divine love and an extension of that love to others. (Piper, "The New Birth Produces Love")

So love has its very origin and source in God, and it is evidence that we have been born of God and are a part of "the family of lovers."

Loving Others Gives Evidence We Know God (1 John 4:7-8)

Not only do those who love with a God-like love give evidence that they have been born of God, but they also demonstrate in an ongoing habit of life that they know God. They don't simply know *about* God, they know Him intimately and personally as Father (1 John 3:1).

If verse 7 is the positive affirmation, verse 8 is the negative warning with an important addendum. If your life is not characterized by a God-like love, a love that even cares for its enemies, then you don't know God. And, by logical extension, you have not been born of God. Why? "Because God is love." John will say this twice (vv. 8,16). It is the very character, essence, and nature of God to love. And, as we will see in verse 10, this means He seeks the best for others even at great cost and expense to Himself.

It is God's nature to love (to give and sacrifice). The truth that "God is love" complements other beautiful statements made about God's nature in the Bible. God is Spirit (John 4:24). God is a consuming fire (Heb 12:29). God is light (1 John 1:5). God is true (1 John 5:20).

"God is love" does not equal "love is God" (a form of pantheistic thinking), any more than "grass is green" means "green is grass." Love does not define God, but God does define love. This is John's beautiful logic: (1) God is love. (2) Those who have been born of God and know God are God's children. (3) God's children have God's nature. (4) God's children therefore will love. Love's source is in God, and as we love like God loves, we give evidence we are connected to the source. We demonstrate by a life of love that we know God.

Love Is Seen in the Atoning Death of Jesus
1 JOHN 4:9-10

It is one thing to talk about love. It is something else to show love. The Christian God is not just a talking God. He is an acting God, a doing God, and a serving God.

I often meet hurting people who are wondering, "Does anyone love me?" They have been abused, abandoned, betrayed, lied to, mistreated, and deeply wounded. You may be like this, where you can barely ask the questions but still you do, "Does anyone love me? Will I ever be loved?"

The good news of the gospel provides a resounding "Yes!" to those questions. You are loved and will always be loved by a God who is love and who wants to shower you, deluge you, with His love. How do we know? He sent His Son. To make sure you do not miss it, John says it twice (vv. 9-10). God sent His Son for you and for me.

God Sent His Son That We Might Live (1 John 4:9)

The phrase "God's love was revealed [made clear, put on display] among us in this way" looks forward to what follows. And this love of God was put on public display "among us." We did not just hear about it, John says; we saw it. We were eyewitnesses. Here is what we know: "God sent His One and Only Son into the world," and He did so for this purpose: "so that we might live through Him."

God sent His only Son. "Only" translates a word (Gk *monogenes*) used five times in the New Testament in reference to Jesus (John 1:14,18; 3:16,18; 1 John 4:9). It means unique, one of a kind. There was and is no one else like this Son. You should hear the words of John 3:16 ringing in your ears.

God sent His Son from heaven because that is where He was, in eternal existence with His Father and in loving communion through the Holy Spirit. Our God was not lonely in need of company. The triune God has existed forever in perfect, loving community and communion. No, our God was not lonely; He was loving. He sent His Son into enemy territory, into a world of sinners on a search and rescue mission. He came looking for us even when we were not looking for Him.

And why did He come? He came "that we might live through Him." This world of humanity was dead with no life or hope (cf. Eph 2:1-3). God sent His Son. This world of humanity was in rebellion against its loving Creator. God sent His Son. This world of humanity was not looking for God and even hated Him. God sent His Son.

What does it mean to "live through Him?" It means to be born of God and to know God. It means to experience His love and share that love with others. It means to enjoy fellowship with the Father, Son, and Holy Spirit. It means to walk in the light, enjoy fellowship with one another, confess and receive forgiveness of sins, walk as He walked, abide in the Word and His will, know the truth, be confident at His second coming, have victory over sin, and so much more. What a life the Son provides!

God Sent His Son That He Might Die (1 John 4:10)

This is one of the most wonderful and important verses in the Bible. It notes the initiative God took in loving us, and it addresses the magnitude of that love in the gift of His Son. God did not send an angel; He sent His Son. God did not send His Son to live; He sent His Son to die. And this was not an ordinary death. Nor was it simply the death of a martyr. It was the death of a Savior dying in our place and bearing our punishment.

As John states "Love consists in this," he again is pointing to what follows. First, God loved us before we loved Him. In fact He loved us when we spurned Him. Second, He proved His love by sending His Son. Paul said something very similar in Romans 5:8: "But God proves His own love for us in that while we were still sinners, Christ died for us!" Third, God sent His Son to be the propitiation (NIV, "atoning sacrifice") for our sins. The word "propitiation" is a rich theological term and one of the most important in the Bible. It is used three other times in the New Testament in the context of Jesus' death on the cross and His work of atonement:

God presented Him as a propitiation through faith in His blood, to demonstrate His righteousness. (Rom 3:25)

Therefore, He had to be like His brothers in every way, so that He could become a merciful and faithful high priest in service to God, to make propitiation for the sins of the people. (Heb 2:17)

He Himself is the propitiation for our sins, and not only for ours, but also for those of the whole world. (1 John 2:2)

The word means to turn away the wrath of God by means of an offering. In ancient pagan religions, human worshippers made the offering to appease an angry deity. The New Testament knows nothing of this. In Christ, God Himself made the satisfaction, the atonement, as He offered Himself in His Son. As 2 Corinthians 5:19 says, "In Christ, God was reconciling the world to Himself, not counting their trespasses against them." And the fact that God provides the satisfaction Himself teaches us several truths about God. Propitiation teaches us that God personally hates sin. Propitiation teaches us that sin is serious. Propitiation teaches us the greatness of God's love in which He provided the offering to turn His wrath away. Propitiation teaches us the truth that Christ's death satisfied the Father and was a substitution for sinners. Propitiation teaches us that God's holiness required satisfaction and that God's love provided satisfaction.

John Stott says it just right in his classic work on the atonement, *The Cross of Christ*:

> It is God himself who in holy wrath needs to be propitiated, God himself who in holy love undertook to do the propitiation, and God himself who in the person of his Son died for the propitiation of our sins. Thus God took his own loving initiative to appease his own righteous anger by bearing it his own self in his own Son when he took our place and died for us. (*The Cross of Christ*, 175)

Likewise, Tim Keller reminds us,

> The gospel is that Jesus lived the life you should have lived and died the death you should have died, in your place, so God can receive you not for your record and sake but for his record and sake. ("Keller on Preaching to a Post-Modern City II")

And Stott again would add,

> For the essence of sin is man substituting himself for God, while the essence of salvation is God substituting himself for man. Man asserts himself against God and puts himself where only God deserves to be; God sacrifices himself for man and puts himself where only man deserves to be. (*The Cross of Christ*, 160)

Love Is Perfected in Us When We Love Others
1 JOHN 4:11-12

It is too often the case that Christians are not known for their love of others. Sometimes the criticisms are unjustified. Unfortunately, at other times we are guilty as charged. Recent research by Gabe Lyons and David Kinnaman reveals we are often seen by the lost as "hyperpolitical, out of touch, pushy in our beliefs, and arrogant"; in particular we are viewed by young Americans who do not attend church as antihomosexual (91%), judgmental (87%), hypocritical (85%), and insensitive to others (70%) (White, *The Church in an Age of Crisis*, 175). And yet,

Jesus said love for others is how people know we are His disciples (John 13:35). He also says to love our enemies and to pray for those who hate us and would harm us if they could (Matt 5:44).

The great and challenging application to these commands is that we must go to those who don't want us there. We must share a gospel they don't want to hear. We must love those who may hate and even kill us in return. Because we are connected to Jesus through the new birth, we must go and live like Jesus among our friends and our enemies.

God's Love for Us Inspires Us to Love Others (1 John 4:11)

When we were in darkness, God sent His light. When we were dead, God sent His life. When we were in sin, God sent His Son. When we were in despair, God sent His love. For the second time in this passage we are addressed as "Dear friends." John is not transitioning to a new subject this time. Rather, he wants to build on and add to his previous words in verses 7-10. He uses a common "greater to lesser" argument. Let me paraphrase: "If God loves us in this way (and He does; just look to the cross of Christ), then we ought naturally—out of gospel gratitude and connection to the very source of love, God—love one another."

John 17:26 is extremely helpful at this point. There Jesus says, "I made Your name known to them and will make it known, so the love You have loved Me with may be in them and I may be in them." Later, in 1 John 4:13-16, John will address more fully the beautiful Trinitarian component to this wonderful life of love.

When John says here "we also must" love one another, I think he means something like this: Live out day-by-day who you are as those who are born of God, know God, and have experienced the love of God in the sacrifice of His Son. We are simply experiencing and enjoying who we are in Christ when we love one another. After all, God's seed is now in us (3:9) and God's Spirit is now in us (3:24). Loving others is just what we do because the love that has rained down on us now fills us as we abide in Him.

Our Love for Others Brings His Love to Perfection (1 John 4:12)

This verse is striking and unexpected in its beginning. The word "seen" is from the Greek word *theaomai* (we get "theater" from it), and it implies a careful observing, a close scrutiny or examination. No person has seen God "up close and personal" in His unveiled essence, glory, and majesty.

To do so would certainly be our death. In the Old Testament, Moses on Mt. Sinai (Exod 33:22-23) and Isaiah in the temple (Isa 6) only saw theophanies, which are visions or revelations of God. They could see and handle this (barely!) without being consumed. If they beheld much more of His essence than that, they would have been vaporized.

John's argument, however, takes a beautiful turn. No one can see God in His essence, but we can see God through the lives of those who demonstrate His love to others. Stott again says it well: Mutual Christian love is the evidence that "the unseen God, who was once revealed in His Son, is now revealed in His people . . . when they love one another" (*The Letters of John*, 164). John makes his point by stating that when we love one another, (1) it is proof that God abides continually in us, and (2) His love (God's love for us; His kind of love) is "perfected," brought to complete maturity. It reaches its intended goal. John's point is twofold. First, I can love others as God loves me because He lives in me. And second, His love will reach its intended goal, which is that I will love others as He loves me. It is a wonderful circle of theological truth that cannot be broken. After all, God is its source, its maintenance, and its perfection. It is all of God from beginning to end.

Conclusion

On June 25, 1967, more than 400 million people in 26 countries watched, via satellite, the Beatles perform the song "All You Need Is Love." They had been asked to come up with a simple song that could be understood by all the nations. While I believe their thesis was incorrect, I can understand why it was the cry of their hearts and that of the rest of the world. Why? Because it is very close to the truth. You see, what we really need is the God who is love! To be precise, what we really need is Jesus, who was sent by the God who is love. What we need is not to be connected to love, but to be connected to Christ, the source of love. And when that happens, real love, supernatural love, will flow like a river from Him into you, and out of you to others. Then you will come to see and know for yourself the wonderful truth, "God is love."

Reflect and Discuss

1. How would you explain the meaning of "love" to a child in a way that child could understand?
2. How is the supernatural love of God different from the superficial idea of love that we so often hold?
3. Why does love have its origin in God? Can unregenerate people truly love? How is the love shown by those born of God different?
4. What is the difference between knowing about God and knowing God personally as Father? Why is love a good test for whether someone knows God?
5. How does John see a bloody cross as the highest expression of love?
6. How is the new life we live in Christ different from just religious ritualism or asceticism?
7. Why is it important to remember that God sent Jesus knowing that He would die? What does this tell us about Jesus' ministry?
8. How would you define propitiation to a group of your peers? What does it tell us about God? About man? Where do we see these themes throughout the rest of Scripture?
9. How can Christians perfect the love of God? Does that mean there is something lacking in Christ's work?
10. What would Christian love look like if Christ's example was truly followed? How can you follow the example of love He displayed on the Cross?

The Power of Love

1 JOHN 4:13-21

Main Idea: God's love in His people gives them assurance of His presence, confidence awaiting judgment, and power to reflect His character in the world.

I. **Love Is an Evidence That We Have the Spirit (4:13-16).**
   A. We abide in the Spirit's presence (4:13).
   B. We confess the Son as Savior (4:14-15).
   C. We know the Father's love (4:16).
II. **Love Gives Us Confidence As We Await the Day of Judgment (4:17-18).**
   A. We can be confident for the future (4:17).
   B. We can be confident with no fear (4:18).
III. **Love Is a Command Because It Reflects God's Character (4:19-21).**
   A. To love God and hate your brother is to live a lie (4:19-20).
   B. To love God and love your brother is to obey God's command (4:21).

Our actions are often determined by our identity—who we are and who we think we are. John wants us to be loving (actions), but first he wants us to know we are loved as those who abide in God through the gift of His Spirit (identity). Have you taken the time to reflect on who you are in Christ? Have you stopped to consider some of the magnificent ways you have been blessed and loved by God? Just meditate a moment on the following:

- Through Christ, I am dead to sin (Rom 6:11).
- Through Christ, I am spiritually alive (Rom 6:11; 1 Cor 15:22).
- Through Christ, I am forgiven (Col 2:13; 1 John 2:12).
- Through Christ, I am declared righteous (1 Cor 1:30; 2 Cor 5:21).
- Through Christ, I am a child of God (Rom 8:16; Phil 2:15).
- Through Christ, I am God's possession (Titus 2:14).
- Through Christ, I am blessed with all spiritual blessings (Eph 1:3).

- Through Christ, I am a citizen of heaven (Phil 3:20).
- Through Christ, I am free from the law (Rom 8:2).
- Through Christ, I am crucified with Him (Gal 2:20).
- Through Christ, I am an heir of God (Rom 8:17).
- Through Christ, I am free from the desires of the flesh (Gal 5:24).
- Through Christ, I am declared blameless and innocent (Phil 2:15).
- Through Christ, I am a light in the world (Matt 5:14-15; Phil 2:15).
- Through Christ, I am victorious over Satan (Luke 10:19).
- Through Christ, I am cleansed from sin (1 John 1:7).
- Through Christ, I am set free from the power of sin (Col 2:11-15).
- Through Christ, I am secure in Him (1 Pet 1:3-5).
- Through Christ, I am at peace with God (Rom 5:1; Phil 4:6-9).
- Through Christ, I am loved by God (1 John 4:10). (Thomas and Wood, *Gospel Coach*, 71–72)

That is an impressive list. It is a supernatural list. It is a list that reveals the power of the Spirit and the power of love, all because "the Father has sent His Son as the world's Savior" (1 John 4:14). Therefore, "if God loved us in this way, we also must love one another" (v. 11).

Loving others as we have been loved by God is not an easy thing to do. Loving and praying for our enemies as Jesus taught us in Matthew 5:43-48 can seem nearly impossible. Even loving our brothers and sisters in Christ can be a real challenge at times. We need some supernatural assistance. We need to remember who we are in Christ and what we have received from the Father. When we do, an amazing thing will happen. We will love others as we have been loved by God. And by the way we love others, we will make visible the invisible God this world so desperately needs to see and come to know. That is indeed the power of love! Three movements in this text unwrap for us what I call "the dynamo of love."

Love Is an Evidence That We Have the Spirit
1 JOHN 4:13-16

These verses are Trinitarian to the core. When we experience the power of divine love, we experience the work and enjoy the fellowship of the triune God. John Piper says, "I think we will love each other and those outside with a distinct, supernatural love when we taste the fellowship of the Trinity" ("Love One Another for Love Is of God"). I like the sound of that.

The Spirit is on display in verse 13. The Son takes center stage in verses 14-15. The Father is highlighted in verses 14-16. God sent His Son to die for us. He sent His Spirit to live in us. Both are gifts of grace. Both are evidences of His amazing love for us. And the love that we now have for God and His children is a revelation of the Holy Spirit who is within us through our relationship with Jesus. Love is certified proof that God now resides in us, not in a pantheistic sense, but through His personal presence.

We Abide in the Spirit's Presence (1 John 4:13)

Verse 13 begins with the phrase "This is how we know." It is interesting and instructive just how many times John uses this phrase in this letter:

2:3 "This is how we are sure that we have come to know Him . . ."

2:5b "This is how we know we are in Him . . ."

3:10 "This is how God's children—and the Devil's children—are made evident . . ."

3:14 "We know that we have passed from death to life . . ."

3:19 "This is how we will know we belong to the truth . . ."

3:24 "And the way we know that He remains in us . . ."

4:2 "This is how you know the Spirit of God . . ."

4:6b "From this we know the Spirit of truth and the spirit of deception . . ."

5:2 "This is how we know that we love God's children . . ."

5:13 "I have written these things to you who believe in the name of the Son of God, so that you may know that you have eternal life."

John wants his readers to know, to be assured of many things. Here he wants them to know they abide in God and God abides in them through the gift of the Holy Spirit, the Third Person of the triune God. Now, how do they know that this mutual abiding in the Spirit is real? Verse 12 provides part of the answer: because "we love one another . . . and His love is perfected in us." A more full description is found in verses 15-16: "Whoever confesses that Jesus is the Son of God—God remains in him and he in God. And we have come to know and to believe the love that God has for us. God is love, and the one who remains in love remains in God, and God remains in him." Putting it all together we know we abide in God and God abides in us because (1) He gave us His Spirit as a grace gift at conversion, (2) we confess Jesus is the Son of God (Savior of the world, 4:14), and (3) we abide in God's love and His love abides in us. God gave us His Spirit, and He will never take Him from us. He is ours now and forever. For all of eternity there will be this mutual indwelling between us and the Holy Spirit. What a blessing! What a gift!

We Confess the Son as Savior (1 John 4:14-15)

Our motivation to obey God's command to love one another (vv. 7,11,12) can become a delight and joy when we look to Christ and soak in what He did for us. Loving others will not spring forth out of guilt, but out of gospel gladness and gratitude. We are not motivated by our failures but by His forgiveness. We are moved to love because of our connection to Christ, who has so lavishly loved us.

These two verses have a strong missionary pulse surging through their veins. In verse 14 John affirms what he has seen as an apostolic witness. In verse 15 he addresses his confession and the blessings that accompany that confession.

Now, what did he observe first hand that he must bear witness to? It is this: "the Father has sent His Son as the world's Savior." Once again John directs us to Jesus and what the Father has accomplished by His Son. In the Son the Father . . .

- revealed the word of life (1:1),
- brought eternal life (1:2),
- cleanses us from all sin (1:7),
- gave us an advocate (2:1),
- propitiates our sins (2:2; 4:10),
- gives us an example to follow (2:6),
- sent the Messiah (2:22-23),
- makes possible the new birth (2:29),
- sent the righteous and sinless One (2:29; 3:4),
- takes away our sin (3:5),
- destroys the work of the Devil (3:8),
- sacrificed His Son (3:16), and
- gives us life (4:9).

To all of this we can shout "Hallelujah! What a Savior!" This is the Savior the Father sent, and this is the Savior we share with a world of seven billion people. It is a world of 16,500 people groups, 6,900 of which are unreached, totaling more than 2.9 billion unreached persons on planet earth (JoshuaProject.net, accessed Feb. 10, 2014). Jesus came to die for this world, and we have the assignment to tell them this good news. But remember what Carl F. H. Henry well said: "The gospel is only good news if it gets there in time." But when it does get there in time and they do hear it and confess it as their heart cry (v. 15), something wonderful happens: they are converted, regenerated, born again, born of God. Beginning with this new birth, God now abides in them, and they now abide in God. Their life is in God and, by the Spirit, God's life is in them. This is true for all who confess Jesus as Savior.

We Know the Father's Love (1 John 4:16)

For the second time in chapter 4 John declares, "God is love" (cf. v. 8). And what a loving God He is! How do we know? We know through the gift of the Spirit, as in verse 13. And we know because of the gift of the Son, as in verses 14-15. So, we know and believe as a settled reality in our souls that the God who is love indeed loves us. Furthermore, as we abide in the love of God, the God of love abides in us! Thus we see faith and love and knowledge working together to assure our hearts that this God of love is our God and Father. Warren Wiersbe says,

> The more we love God, the more we understand the love of God. And the more we understand His love, the easier it is to trust Him. After all, when you know someone intimately and love him sincerely, you have no problem putting your confidence in him. (*Be Real*, 150–51)

This is indeed a "Father God" we know we can trust.

Love Gives Us Confidence As We Await the Day of Judgment
1 JOHN 4:17-18

John shifts gears and changes direction at this point. He wants to bring into the discussion both the subject of judgment (v. 17) and the subject of fear (v. 18). Loving others out of gratitude for how we have been loved in Christ has consequences not only for the present, but also for the future. The argument John has built to this point is powerful. It runs something like this: loving others (vv. 7,11-12), possessing the Spirit (v. 13), confessing the Son (v. 15), and mutually abiding in God and His love (vv. 15-16) bring God's love to its full and intended goal, its 'perfect purpose in our lives. Two wonderful purposes of that goal are confidence when I stand before God on judgment day (v. 17) and the complete absence of fear at that time (v. 18). How is this possible? The answer is because on that day when you stand before God He will see you as He sees His dear Son. The love of God will have done its perfect work as it is applied to that day when we stand before God.

We Can Be Confident for the Future (1 John 4:17)

Love has an intended goal. The word "perfected" carries the idea of completion, being brought to maturity. Abiding in the love of God gives us "confidence," boldness, for the judgment day. Judgment day is something every person should consider with healthy seriousness. It is real, and it is coming. No one spoke more often or more vividly of judgment than Jesus. The word "hell" (Gk *Gehenna*) is used 12 times in the New Testament; all but one occurrence comes from the mouth of Jesus (cf. Jas 3:6). The very purpose of His coming was to help people be prepared for that day. John says we can not only be ready, but we can be confident. Why? Because on that day "we are as He is in this world." What does John mean by this? I think the answer is something like this: Because we are in Christ—abiding in Him and He abiding in us—we stand in relation to God and the world the same way Christ does. John MacArthur says it beautifully:

> This stunning statement means the Father treats the saints the same way He does His Son Jesus Christ. God clothes believers with the righteousness of Christ (Rom. 3:21-22; 2 Cor. 5:21; Phil. 3:9), and He grants the Son's perfect love (Matt. 9:36; John 10:11,14-16; 13:1; 14:21) and obedience (cf. John 4:34; 5:30; 18:37). Someday believers will stand before God's throne as confidently as their Lord and Savior does. When they reach that final accounting, they will see the fulfillment of 1 John 3:2b, "We [believers] know that when He appears, we will be like Him, because we will see Him just as He is." (*1–3 John*, 171)

We Can Be Confident with No Fear (1 John 4:18)

The phrase "no fear" is quite popular. A clothing brand by that name was started in 1989, opened its first retail store in 2000, launched an energy drink in 2003, and filed for bankruptcy in 2011. Apparently its staying power and shelf-life were limited.

Such is not the case with the love of God. Verse 17 states this truth positively, and verse 18 states it negatively. When God's love has reached its intended goal and accomplished its perfect work, fear before God is driven out and the dread of punishment is vanquished. This is one of the joys and blessings of knowing God as Father. This holy and righteous Judge is also our *Abba*, Father. In contrast, those who do live in fear of future punishment give evidence that something is wrong, that God's perfecting work of love has not done its work in their lives. So, out of gospel gratitude for who you are in Christ, love others as He has loved you. The threat of punishment will disappear. The fear of punishment will evaporate. Love never fears judgment or punishment. It is bold. It is confident.

Love Is a Command Because It Reflects God's Character
1 JOHN 4:19-21

In Matthew 22:36-40 Jesus addressed the two great commands: loving God and loving others. There He made what many would see as a startling statement. He said that loving your neighbor is "like" loving God. Now in our text, John will add that you cannot love God without loving your neighbor. In fact to say you love God while hating a fellow human being just will not work. In fact, it turns you into a liar and gives evidence that you actually don't love God either.

To Love God and Hate Your Brother Is to Live a Lie (1 John 4:19-20)

Verse 19 is one of the most simple and straightforward verses in the Bible. The theological order is important. "We love." Why? "Because He first loved us." God took the initiative, not us. Our love finds its origin in God's love. He loves us, and the love that now abides in us and has been perfected in us overflows in loving words and actions to others. The Father's prior love is source and cause for our love of others. If I am not loving others as I ought, then I do not know God's love as I should. That, in essence, is John's argument in verse 20.

Once again we encounter an "If anyone says" statement (cf. 1:6,8,10; 2:4,6,9). Here the person under examination says one thing but does another that contradicts his words. With his lips he says, "I love God," but in his heart (and actions) he "hates his brother." John's verdict is quick, clear, and to the point: "He is a liar."

John's logic is flawless. It is what we call a "lesser to greater" analogy. The gist is that if you do not have the ability to love the brother you can see, it is impossible for you to love the God you have not seen. If you do not manage to love His creatures, then you cannot love the Creator. If you do not have the capacity to love His children, then you cannot love their Father. John Stott is right when he notes, "It is obviously easier to love and serve a visible man than an invisible God, and if we fail in the easier task, it is absurd to claim success in the harder" (*The Letters of John*, 173). God calls us to walk in the truth. That involves loving God and loving others.

To Love God and Love Your Brother Is to Obey God's Command (1 John 4:21)

Verse 21 is basically a summation of John's discourse on love that began back in 4:7. It also, in a very wise theological strategy, looks to the words of Jesus to settle the issue and answer any remaining questions or objections someone might raise.

"And we have this command from Him" refers again to the words of Jesus concerning the greatest command, found in Matthew 22:37-39 and Mark 12:30-31. What Jesus gave us was a command. It was not a suggestion or recommendation. It was not just a good idea we might consider. If we truly love God, then we must truly love our brother as well. The Godward and human-directed aspects of love cannot be divided. They cannot be separated. They really are the bookends of all the commands. They are the "heads and tails" of the same coin of love. Our ability to actually love God is wedded to the reality of our love for fellow human beings. And such a love is not sporadic or periodic. It is not occasional. It is continual. It reflects and demonstrates for all to see the love of God for sinners that was put on public display on a bloody Roman cross when "the Father . . . sent His Son as the world's Savior" (1 John 4:14). As D. Edmond Hiebert has wisely observed, "Since God's love is no longer visible in the presence of the incarnate Christ here on earth, God is manifesting His love as it is now displayed in His people" ("An Exposition of 1 John 4:7-21," 83).

Conclusion

In Luke 7:47 Jesus says that those who have been forgiven much will love much. We have been forgiven much. We have been forgiven everything we have ever done wrong or ever will do wrong. So, living in the power of that truth made possible through the perfect atoning death of Jesus (1 John 4:10), let's love wholly the God whom we have not seen (but someday will), and let's love well the brother and sister we do see today. There really is supernatural power in love. If you have any doubts, just look to the cross! The crucified God declares it to be so.

Reflect and Discuss

1. Explain the connection between identity and action when it comes to love. Why must identity come first?
2. How is receiving and showing love related to the Trinity?
3. Why is the mutual abiding between Christians and the Holy Spirit such a blessing? How do we know if this is real in our own lives?
4. How has your increasing love for God increased your understanding of God's love for you?
5. How does abiding in the love of God give us confidence when we face judgment? How does it reassure us for the future?
6. Why does love cast out fear? What does fear reveal about our relationship to God?
7. Why does John combine loving God with loving your neighbor? Which is more important?
8. Why is it impossible to love an invisible God if you do not love your brother?
9. How is the command to love God and neighbor seen throughout the Scriptures?

The Birthmarks of the Children of God

1 JOHN 5:1-5

Main Idea: True Christians will display evidence of being God's children, including right beliefs about God and holy living before God.

I. We Believe That Jesus Is the Messiah (5:1).
II. We Have Been Born of God (5:1,4).
III. We Love the Father and His Family (5:1-2).
IV. We Obey His Commands (5:2-3).
V. We Have Overcome the World (5:4).
VI. We Believe Jesus Is the Son of God (5:5).

It is very often the case that children follow in their parents' footsteps. We often hear the statements "like father, like son" or "she is just like her mother." In addition, it is also the case that children usually bear a striking resemblance to their mom, dad, or both. Someone may say, "He is the spitting image of his dad. He has his dad's eyes/nose/chin." Our daughters-in-law are fond of pointing out in their children what they call "the Akin mouth"! I am not quite sure if they mean their mouth is similar to their dad and mine or that they talk a lot like their dad and granddaddy! Either way they are acknowledging family resemblance or "birthmarks" that give evidence of those to whom they belong.

In the letter of 1 John, the last living apostle has repeatedly drawn attention to three overarching birthmarks of the children of God. They are right belief (the doctrinal mark), right love (the moral mark), and right behavior (the ethical or social mark). Now in 1 John 5:1-5 he is going to draw out necessary implications of these three birthmarks and highlight six specific identifying evidences that a person is a child of God. John wants true believers to be assured that they are children of God, and he is fully aware of the fact that there are spiritual deceivers in their midst who could raise questions and cast doubts (2:26). John wants believers to have a rock-solid assurance that they have been born again, that they belong to Jesus, and that they can enjoy right now the gift of eternal life (5:13).

John Piper says the evidences of the new birth could probably be boiled down to two: faith and love ("Regeneration, Faith, Love"). I think he is right, and here we see how the apostle John develops these ideas to assure us we are in the family, the family of God.

We Believe That Jesus Is the Messiah
1 JOHN 5:1

Once again John raises the doctrinal or Christological issue. We are reminded that true Christianity always comes back to Jesus—who He is and what you believe about Him. John will begin and end this section with a Christological affirmation (vv. 1,5). I find it fascinating that he bookends this text with the two-part confession of the apostle Peter in Matthew 16:16: "You are the Messiah, the Son of the living God." In 1 John 5:1 we must believe Jesus is the Messiah (Christ), and in verse 5 we must confess Him as the Son of God.

John begins with an all inclusive word: "Everyone." No one is excluded. All must embrace and articulate the statement that follows. The word "believes" speaks of continuous action. Everyone who "is believing" is the idea. Adrian Rogers said it well: "The assurance of my salvation comes not from the fact that I did trust Christ but that I am trusting Christ for my salvation" (*Adrianisms*, 186). And what must we believe? We must believe "that Jesus is the Messiah." We must believe—trust in the truth—that Jesus of Nazareth is the Messiah, the Christ, the hoped-for and promised deliverer. Such a confession is a birthmark that we have been born of God and that we are children of God.

The London pastor and preacher Charles Spurgeon fleshes out the theological implications of this confession of faith as only he could. He says,

> The faith intended in the text *evidently rests upon a Person*—upon Jesus. "Whoever believes that Jesus is the Christ is born of God." It is not belief about a *doctrine*, nor an *opinion*, nor a *formula*, but belief concerning a *Person*. Translate the words, "Whoever believes that Jesus is the Christ," and they stand thus—"Whoever believes that the Savior is the Anointed, is born of God." . . .
>
> What is meant by, "Jesus is the Christ," or, Jesus is the Anointed? First, that He is the Prophet. Secondly, that He is the Priest. Thirdly, that He is the King of the Church, for in all

these three senses He is the Anointed. Now, I may ask myself
this question—Do I this day believe that Jesus is the great
Prophet anointed of God to reveal to me the way of salvation?
Do I accept Him as my Teacher and admit that He has the
Words of eternal life? If I so believe, I shall obey His Gospel
and possess eternal life.

Do I accept Him to be, from now, on the Revealer of God
to my soul, the Messenger of the Covenant, the Anointed
Prophet of the Most High? But He is also a Priest. Now a priest
is ordained from among men to offer sacrifices—do I firmly
believe that Jesus was ordained to offer His one Sacrifice for
the sins of mankind, by the offering of which sacrifice, once
and for all, He has finished atonement and made complete
expiation? Do I accept His Atonement as an atonement for *me*,
and receive His death as an expiation upon which I rest my
hope for forgiveness of all my transgressions?

Do I, in fact, believe Jesus to be the one sole, only
propitiating Priest, and accept Him to act as Priest for me? If so,
then I have in part believed that Jesus is the Anointed. But He
is also King, and if I desire to know whether I possess the right
faith, I further must ask myself, "Is Jesus, who is now exalted
in Heaven, who once bled on the cross, is He King to me? Is
His law my law? Do I desire entirely to submit myself to His
government? Do I hate what He hates, and love what He loves?
Do I live to praise Him? Do I, as a loyal subject, desire to see His
kingdom come and His will done on earth as it is in Heaven?"

My dear Friend, if you can heartily and earnestly say, "I
accept Jesus Christ of Nazareth to be Prophet, Priest, and King
to me because God has anointed Him to exercise those three
offices. And in each of these three Characters I unfeignedly
trust Him," then, dear Friend, you have the faith of God's elect,
for it is written, "He that believes that Jesus is the Christ is born
of God." ("Faith and Regeneration," emphasis in original)

We Have Been Born of God
1 JOHN 5:1,4

John will allude to the new birth three times in these verses. It is a theme
he began in 2:29 and will complete in 5:18. There is little doubt he got the

idea from Jesus in John 3, where Jesus told the religious leader Nicodemus, "Unless someone is born again, he cannot see the kingdom of God" (John 3:3). In these verses John makes three observations about the new birth and the evidences related to this birthmark. First, those who have been born of God give witness concerning their new birth by confessing that Jesus is the Messiah (v. 1). Second, those who have been born of God give witness concerning their new birth by loving Father God and His children (v. 1). Third, those who have been born of God give witness concerning their new birth by continually overcoming the world (v. 4).

Being "born of God" is a biblical birthmark or description of a Christian. It also is designated in Scripture as being "born again" or "born from above" (John 3:3,7; 1 Pet 1:23) and "regeneration" (Titus 3:5). It is not an optional or secondary experience for a child of God. It is essential and initiatory. Jesus said in John 3:7, "You must be born again." To be a Christian is to be born again or "born of God." If you have not been born again, you are not a Christian. However, if you will simply trust Jesus as your Messiah—believing Him to be the very Son of God who lived the life you should have lived but didn't, died the death you should have died but now do not have to, and was raised from the dead to give you a salvation you do not deserve—you will indeed experience the supernatural work of God that is the new birth. Being born of God and believing in Jesus are intertwined in the Bible and cannot be separated. "Born of God" looks to the work of God in transforming our hearts. "Believing in Jesus" looks to the human response as we hear and believe the gospel. In this new birth God does not just give you a new name; He gives you a new nature. He gives you the very nature of God Himself as you enter into His family.

Jesus did not come to die on a bloody cross to make us kinder and nicer persons. He came to dramatically, personally, radically, and eternally transform us and make us new people. It is by the new birth that He accomplishes this glorious work. Therefore, you must be born again. Have you experienced the new birth?

We Love the Father and His Family
1 JOHN 5:1-2

Doctrinal excellence, a bold faith, evangelistic fervor, and a generous hand are all good things. However, they are not what matters most to

God. The one thing that He desires more than anything else is that we love Him. Without love for God, even the good things we do have no value in His eyes.

In these two verses we see that our love for God is multidimensional. It flows to the Father but then its streams branch out in several directions. The word "love" appears more than 30 times in 1 John 4:7–5:3. It occurs five times here in verses 1-3.

The new birth of regeneration brings us into a relationship with God as Father. This Father first loved us and now we love Him (4:19) for who He is and what He has done for us in Christ (4:10). However, we not only love the Father, we also love the family the Father is building. We will love our brothers and sisters, "the one[s] born of Him" (5:1). But John then makes an interesting statement in verse 2 that at first seems out of order. He says we can "know that we love God's children when we love God and obey His commands." But is it out of order? Shouldn't he be saying that we know we love God because we love His children? I don't think so. I think John's point actually is grounded in Jesus' teaching on the two great commands (Matt 22:36-40). My love for others is the natural complement and companion to my "first love" for God. When I love God, I will keep His commands. And keeping His commands involves loving others, His daughters and sons in particular. Furthermore, verse 3 informs us that obeying the command to love one another will not be burdensome. It will be a joy and a delight because the new birth makes it the natural thing to do. And our love for the Father inspires and motivates us to love those He loves and to love them as He loves us.

John's argument has tremendous practical application. First, it will protect us from sentimental and emotional understandings of love that leave God's character and commands out of the picture. Second, because my love for God guides my love for others, I will seek their ultimate good, not that which is temporal and passing. I will not seek to make others comfortable while neglecting their greatest need, which is eternal salvation in Christ. I may clothe, educate, and feed them, which are all good undertakings, but I will strive above all other acts of kindness to help them come to know, love, and trust in Jesus as the Son of God and their personal Messiah (v. 1). After all, as our Lord said in Mark 8:36, "For what does it benefit a man to gain the whole world yet lose his life?"

We Obey His Commands
1 JOHN 5:2-3

John returns to the theme of obedience to the commands of God (cf. 2:4,7-8; 3:22-24). Though he knew that loving God and obeying God were distinguishable, he also knew that they were inseparable (John 14:15). Here he adds a new perspective on obedience that I believe is liberating. It is found at the end of verse 3, where he says that God's commands "are not a burden." How does that work itself out? John is saying that in the new birth I receive a new nature. With this new nature comes new affections, passions, treasures, and values. Because I now love God instead of hating Him, I treasure and value Him above everyone and everything else. And because I treasure and value Him above everyone and everything else, I delight in obeying Him. Now I find His commands not to be a burden, but a blessing. They are not drudgery, they are a delight. John Piper is right: "What you desire to do with your whole heart is not burdensome to do" ("Regeneration, Faith, Love"). My heart desires to love and obey my Lord.

In the Psalms we repeatedly find the joyful testimonies of regenerate hearts as they sing of their joy in doing the will of the Lord and obeying His commands.

How happy is the man who does not follow the advice of the wicked or take the path of sinners or join a group of mockers! Instead, his delight is in the Lord's instruction, and he meditates on it day and night.
(Ps 1:1-2)

Let those who want my vindication shout for joy and be glad; let them continually say, "The Lord be exalted. He takes pleasure in His servant's well-being." (Ps 35:27)

Take delight in the Lord, and He will give you your heart's desires.
(Ps 37:4)

I delight to do Your will, my God; Your instruction lives within me.
(Ps 40:8)

Hallelujah! Happy is the man who fears the Lord, taking great delight in His commands. (Ps 112:1)

I rejoice in the way revealed by Your decrees as much as in all riches.
(Ps 119:14)

I will delight in Your statutes; I will not forget Your word.
(Ps 119:16)

Your decrees are my delight and my counselors. (Ps 119:24)

Help me stay on the path of Your commands, for I take pleasure in it.
(Ps 119:35)

I delight in Your commands, which I love. (Ps 119:47)

*Their hearts are hard and insensitive, but I delight in Your
instruction.* (Ps 119:70)

*May Your compassion come to me so that I may live, for Your
instruction is my delight.* (Ps 119:77)

*Trouble and distress have overtaken me, but Your commands are my
delight.* (Ps 119:143)

I long for Your salvation, Lord, and Your instruction is my delight.
(Ps 119:174)

Jerry Bridges says it quite well: "Love provides the motive for obeying the commands of the law, but the law provides specific direction for exercising love" (*Transforming Grace*, 111). Loving God rightly, therefore, is not just external behavior and outward obedience. It is a longing to do His will from the heart, out of gospel gratitude for who He is and what He has done for us in Jesus. It is not an "I have to" obedience. It is an "I want to" obedience. I love to obey this King!

We Have Overcome the World
1 JOHN 5:4

The theme of verse 4 is made clear by the repetition of the word "conquer" (also in v. 5). Both "conquer" and "victory" come from the same Greek word, *nike*, which is also the name of the Greek goddess of victory, speed, and strength. Nike's Roman name was "Victoria," and she unsurprisingly has wings in most paintings and statutes.

The one (HCSB translates as the substantive adjective as "whatever") who has been born of God conquers—is continually victorious—over the world. This is a fifth authenticating mark of the children of God. John provided a description of "the world" (three times in vv. 4-5) in 1 John 2:16. It is characterized by the trio of "the lust of the flesh, the lust of the eyes, and the pride in one's lifestyle." Here, in addition to love, he points to another spiritual weapon that grants us victory over the weapons of the world in our spiritual battles: "our faith."

I love the beautiful balance we see as John weds the new birth (God's sovereign work) with our faith (human responsibility). Let's try and put all this together. By means of the new birth (vv. 1,4), which is wedded to our faith in Jesus as the Messiah (v. 1) and the Son of God (v. 5), the power of the world's desires and aspirations is broken and we gain victory over them. The world is no longer my passion; God is! Sinful desires and attractions are no longer beautiful; God and His will are.

Overcomers, via the new birth and faith in Christ, are no longer consumed by what they don't have (lust of the flesh and of the eyes) or what they do have (pride in lifestyle; 2:16). That spell has been broken. The shackles have come loose. The blinders have been removed. We no longer pine after and love stuff. Rather, with new holy affections, we pine after and love God. The new birth makes all of this possible and faith gives us the eyes to see it! Again, John Piper says it so well:

> Faith sees that Jesus is better. That is why faith conquers the world. The world held us in bondage by the power of its desires. But now our eyes have been opened by the new birth to see the superior desirability of Jesus. Jesus is better than the desires of the flesh, and better then the desires of the eyes, and better than the riches that strangle us with greed and pride (Mark 4:19) ("Regeneration, Faith, Love") .

Jesus is indeed superior, and faith is the victory that overcomes the world. Faith was at the beginning, it is with us today, and it will be with us to the end. It is a distinguishing birthmark that says I am a child of God.

We Believe Jesus Is the Son of God
1 JOHN 5:5

Adrian Rogers said, "Faith in faith is just positive thinking, but faith in Jesus is salvation" (*Adrianisms*, 173). John brings us full circle and back to Jesus. In verse 1, those who confess Him as the Messiah give evidence that they have "been born of God." Now in verse 5 those who believe that Jesus is the Son of God understand that this faith commitment is the means whereby they gain victory and overcome the world.

"Son of God" is an important title for Jesus in the Bible. It informs us that He is more than a man. He is also God. He is the God-man. His name "Jesus" identifies Him as a man. "Son of God" identifies Him as God. He has both the nature of humanity as Jesus and the nature of God as the Son of God. He came from God, and He is God. He is the eternal Son who always has existed and always will exist as the Second Person of the triune God.

The birthmark of a child of God is that he believes that Jesus is the Son of God and that only Jesus is the Son of God. This believing, this faith, is both particular and persevering. Jesus and only Jesus is the object of this faith confession. And this confession is continuous and ongoing. "Believe" is a present tense verb noting continuous action. This is not a one-time belief. It is a lifetime belief! And it is a personal and individual belief. No one else can believe for me. No one else can believe for you. You must believe the good news of the gospel for yourself. You must trust Jesus Christ the Son of God for yourself.

John 3:36 says, "The one who believes in the Son has eternal life, but the one who refuses to believe in the Son will not see life; instead, the wrath of God remains on him." I would urge you, plead with you, even beg you: choose Jesus. Choose life. It will not just be your best life now. It will be your best life forever and ever!

Conclusion

The Lübeck Cathedral is a Lutheran church building that was begun in 1173 and completed around 1230. A famous inscription is written on one of the walls:

> Ye call Me Master and obey Me not,
> Ye call Me Light and see Me not,
> Ye call Me Way and walk Me not,
> Ye call Me Life and desire Me not,
> Ye call Me Wise and follow Me not,
> Ye call Me Fair and love Me not,
> Ye call Me Rich and ask Me not,
> Ye call Me Eternal and seek Me not,
> Ye call Me Gracious and trust Me not,
> Ye call Me Noble and serve Me not,
> Ye call Me Mighty and honor Me not,

Ye call Me Just and fear Me not,
If I condemn you, blame Me not.

I have good news: Jesus is indeed all these things and more. And He
does not want to condemn you. The fact is, He already experienced
your condemnation for you when He died as an atoning sacrifice for
your sins (2:2; 4:10). He has something so much better for you than
condemnation. He wants you to believe that He is the Messiah, the Son
of God, and He wants you to experience spiritual new birth. He wants
to change your heart so that you might delight in loving the Father and
the family of God. He wants to inflame you with passion for His glory
so that you desire to keep His commands. He wants to fill you with faith
so that you overcome the obstacles and temptations the world throws at
you. This is what the Son of God wants for you. He wants you to bear in
your life and in your soul the birthmarks that you are a child of God.

Reflect and Discuss

1. Why is a confession of Jesus as the Messiah necessary for being in
   God's family? Is it possible to be a Christian and to waver on this
   issue?
2. How does a confession of Jesus as the Savior help with assurance
   in the Christian life? Is an ongoing confession more or less biblical
   than looking to a past decision for assurance?
3. Why is the new birth so important for the Christian? How does the
   new birth relate to repentance and faith?
4. Why must we maintain a connection between God's love and His
   commands? What is the danger of separating them?
5. Loving others without reference to loving God leads to a distorted
   understanding of love. What are some ways love can be distorted?
6. Do you consider obedience a joy or a burden? What can you do to
   make it more of a joy?
7. What does it mean for believers to have conquered the world? What
   role does faith play?
8. How do some people confuse faith in faith with faith in Jesus? What
   is the difference?
9. First John 5:5 says that the one who believes that Jesus is the Son of
   God conquers the world. James 2:19 says that the demons believe
   there is one God. How are these two examples of belief different?

Six Superlative Witnesses That Jesus Is the Son of God

1 JOHN 5:6-12

Main Idea: Christians can be certain that Jesus is God's Son because God has provided several witnesses that testify to His divine nature, giving hope and assurance to God's children.

I. We Have the Witness of His Baptism (5:6-8).
II. We Have the Witness of His Crucifixion (5:6-8).
III. We Have the Witness of the Holy Spirit (5:6-8).
IV. We Have the Witness of the Father (5:9-10).
V. We Have the Witness of Our Conversion (5:10).
VI. We Have the Witness of Eternal Life (5:11-12).

Bertrand Russell lived from 1872–1970. He was a well-known atheistic philosopher who authored more than 100 books, wrote a three-volume autobiography, and was awarded the Nobel Prize for Literature in 1950. One of his best-known books is *Why I Am Not a Christian* (1927). In it he argued that all organized religions are the residue of the barbaric past, and they dwindle to mere hypocritical superstitions and have no basis in reality. On one occasion Russell was asked what he would say to God if he found himself standing before Him. Russell's answer: "I probably would ask, 'Sir, why did you not give me better evidence?'" (Rosten, "Bertrand Russell and God," 26).

The apostle John would disagree with Russell when it comes to the issue of evidence. As an eyewitness of the life, passion, and resurrection of Jesus, the last living apostle would testify that there is abundant and overwhelming evidence that Jesus is the Son of God, and therefore God exists. The problem is not with the evidence. The problem is with the sinful and unbelieving heart. Charles Spurgeon says it well:

> Christianity puts forth very lofty claims. She claims to be the
> true faith and the only true one. She avows her teachings
> to be Divine and therefore Infallible, while for her great
> Teacher, the Son of God, she demands Divine worship and the
> unreserved confidence and obedience of men. Her commands

are issued to every creature and though, at present, her authority is rejected by millions of mankind, she confidently looks forward to a time when the Truth of God shall obtain universal dominion and Jesus the Lord shall take unto Himself His great power and reign. Now, to justify such high claims, the Gospel ought to produce strong evidence, and it does. It does not lack for external evidences, these are abundant. ("The Three Witnesses")

In these verses a courtroom setting is easily imagined. Some form of the Greek word *martus*, translated "testify," "testimony," or "give testimony," occurs no less than ten times. John places in the dock six witnesses who will testify to the fact that Jesus of Nazareth is the Son of God who gives the gift of eternal life to all who trust in Him. These six witnesses have different but complementary perspectives. And their witness is comprehensive, building a powerful case. John makes his argument by drawing attention to the career of Jesus, from His baptism to His crucifixion. He invites the other persons of the triune God to give their testimony. He even extends an invitation to those of us who have been converted through faith in Jesus (v. 5) to tell our story as well. Open-minded, free-thinking people should at least examine the evidence. They may be surprised just how strong the case is for the verdict that Jesus is God in the flesh (John 1:14,18).

We Have the Witness of His Baptism
1 JOHN 5:6-8

The first witness that John calls to the stand is the witness of Jesus' baptism. The word "water" occurs four times in verses 6-8. Some see this as a reference to the water of physical birth, the water that flowed from our Lord's side when He was pierced on the cross (John 19:34-35), or even the two sacraments or ordinances of baptism (water) and the Lord's Supper (blood). This last perspective was held by both Martin Luther and John Calvin. However, the historical context of refuting the false teachings of Cerinthus, who said the Christ-spirit descended on the man Jesus at His baptism but abandoned Him on the cross, points strongly in the direction that John had the baptism of Jesus in mind.

The baptism of Jesus is so important it is found in all four Gospels (Matt 3:13-17; Mark 1:9-11; Luke 3:21-23; John 1:29-34). Here the triune

God is revealed and Jesus is anointed for His public ministry. Matthew 3:16-17 records it this way:

> *After Jesus was baptized, He went up immediately from the water. The heavens suddenly opened for Him, and He saw the Spirit of God descending like a dove and coming down on Him. And there came a voice from heaven: "This is My beloved Son. I take delight in Him."*

The Father's declaration combines words from Psalm 2:7, a messianic psalm, with Isaiah 42:1, the first of the Servant Songs. Jesus is indeed the anointed Son who will be a King. However, He will be a suffering King, a Servant King. This is the witness of His Father at His baptism.

Some have pointed out that, being sinless, Jesus had no need of being baptized. He does not belong there. And that is true. He no more belongs at a baptism for repentance than He does on a cross for sinners. In both events He identifies Himself with the sinners He came to save. Our Lord's baptism says, "Look at the Holy Spirit of God descending on Him and anointing Him." It says, "Listen to the voice of the Father and His announcement concerning Him." Jesus was not a mere man. He is the Son of God who is the Lamb of God who takes away the sin of the world (John 1:29).

We Have the Witness of His Crucifixion
1 JOHN 5:6-8

The second witness that the apostle calls to the stand is the crucifixion of Christ. This is represented by the word "blood," which occurs three times in verses 6-8. The work of our Savior was initiated at His baptism and it was finished by His bloody death on the cross. Jesus, Himself, said from the cross in John 19:30, "It is finished!"

When Jesus Christ died on the cross as an atoning sacrifice for the sins of the world, His Father again provided significant witnesses concerning the event. There was darkness across the land from noon until three o'clock (Matt 27:45), and "the curtain of the sanctuary was split in two from top to bottom" (Matt 27:51). There was an earthquake (Matt 27:51). A number of Old Testament saints were raised and appeared to many as the first fruits of resurrection life for all who trust in Jesus (Matt 27:52-53). And these events led a hardened Roman centurion to exclaim, "This man really was God's Son!" (Matt 27:54; Mark 15:39). Jesus of Nazareth was not God's special agent who was adopted at His baptism but abandoned at the cross. He was and is the eternal Son of God who entered this world in time and space and died as our propitiation (1 John 2:2; 4:10). His death was not an accident. It was not an act of martyrdom. It was a divine, saving substitution for sinners with redeeming value and worth.

Though modern persons might articulate their rejection of Christ and His atoning death on the cross differently than those in the first century, the bottom line is the same. They say that Jesus of Nazareth suffering a brutal bloody death has no redemptive value and bears no significance for my salvation. Delores Williams represents this perspective when she says, "There is nothing divine in the blood of the cross" (*Sisters in the Wilderness*, 176). Others will even charge that the biblical portrayal of our Lord's death is better viewed as "cosmic child abuse" (Chalke and Mann, *The Lost Message of Jesus*, 182). And still others believe we pursue a wiser course of theological discourse by offering to modern persons what David Powlison calls the "therapeutic gospel," a gospel that gives people what they want and promotes their welfare and temporal happiness. As Powlison says, "It does not want the King of Heaven to come down. It does not attempt to change people into lovers of God, given the truth of who Jesus is, what he is like, what he does" ("The Therapeutic Gospel," 5).

But the cross says the King of Heaven *has* come down, and that God *was* in Christ reconciling the world unto Himself (2 Cor 5:21). This is the true and biblical witness of our Lord's crucifixion. Praise His name, He did come to die for us, and He did come to change us!

We Have the Witness of the Holy Spirit
1 JOHN 5:6-8

The third witness invited to testify to the fact that Jesus is the Son of God is the Holy Spirit of God. He is referenced three times in verses 6-8. In verse 6 the Bible says the Spirit provides a consistent and continuous witness that Jesus is the Messiah, and He does so because "the Spirit is the truth." Jesus said the exact same thing about the Holy Spirit in John 15:26: "When the Counselor comes, the One I will send to you from the Father—the Spirit of truth who proceeds from the Father—He will testify about Me." John MacArthur points out,

> The Father also testified to the Son through the ministry
> of the Spirit, who is the truth (cf. John 14:17; 15:26; 16:13).

The Holy Spirit is the Spirit of truth in that He is true and, therefore, the source and revealer of divine truth (1 Peter 1:12; cf. Acts 1:16; 28:25; Heb. 3:7; 10:15-17), particularly about Jesus Christ (John 15:26). The Spirit was involved at Jesus' conception (Matt. 1:18,20; Luke 1:35), baptism (Matt. 3:16), temptation (Mark 1:12, Luke 4:1), and throughout His ministry. Peter said to those gathered in Cornelius's house, "You know of Jesus of Nazareth, how God anointed Him with the Holy Spirit and with power, and how He went about doing good and healing all who were oppressed by the devil, for God was with Him" (Acts 10:38; cf. Matt. 12:28; Luke 4:14; John 3:34). Because the Holy Spirit empowered Jesus for ministry, to attribute Christ's miraculous works to Satan was to blaspheme the Holy Spirit (Mark 3:28-30). Jesus always did the will of the Father in the power of the Spirit. (*1–3 John*, 195)

The threefold witness of the water (baptism), blood (cross), and Spirit agree (1 John 5:8). This reflects the Old Testament expectation in Deuteronomy 19:15 where the Bible says, "One witness cannot establish any wrongdoing or sin against a person, whatever that person has done. A fact must be established by the testimony of two or three witnesses." In verse 8 the Spirit is mentioned first because it is He who testifies to us through the water and the blood. But all three are in agreement: Jesus is the Messiah, the Son of God. Pastor James Merritt addresses well this ministry of the Holy Spirit as He testifies to the Son: "The witness of the Spirit is God's witness to us, in us, and through us. Just as the arrow of a compass always points towards the North, the Spirit of God always points to Jesus" ("Do You Know for Sure"). Jesus summarized the Spirit's work in John 16:14: "He will glorify Me."

We Have the Witness of the Father
1 JOHN 5:9-10

John continues his parade of witnesses, calling to the stand at this point the strongest witness of all: God the Father. The "testimony" of the Father resounds again and again in verses 9-10 as the apostle employs what we call a "lesser to greater" argument. In the everyday affairs of life, "we accept the testimony of men." In the Jewish context, as we have noted, the testimony of two or three witnesses was necessary and sufficient to confirm something as true (Deut 17:6; 19:15). If that is so, how much more should we believe God Himself, especially when He has just supplied His own threefold witness of the Spirit, water, and blood (v. 8)? The testimony of God is indeed greater—superior in source, status, and significance—than the testimony of any human persons. It is more reliable and trustworthy because it comes from the God, who cannot lie (Heb 6:18).

The testimony given by God is a testimony "He has given about His Son" (v. 9). I think John is saying that the abiding testimony of Jesus' baptism, His crucifixion, and that of the Holy Spirit is God's historical witness that Jesus is His Son. Never did God give such a witness concerning anyone else in all of history. The Father's witness concerning His Son is singular and unique. Therefore, it demands a response from each and every one of us. Neutrality and indecision is not an option. In fact, to not believe that Jesus is the Son of God is to not believe God and to make Him "a liar, because [you have] not believed in the testimony God has given about His Son" (v. 10). John says that believing in Jesus as the Son of God is equivalent to accepting God the Father's testimony about His Son. To reject Jesus as God's Son is equivalent to charging God with perjury. It is that simple, and John is that straightforward. Again, Spurgeon is our helper:

> God is to be believed if all men contradict him. "Let God be true, and every man a liar." One word of God ought to sweep away ten thousand words of men, whether they be philosophers of today or sages of antiquity. God's word is against them all, for he knows infallibly. Of his own Son he knows as none else can; of our condition before him he knows; of the way to pardon us he knows. There is nothing in God that could lead him to err or make a mistake—and it were blasphemy to suppose that he would mislead us. It were an insult to him, such as we may not venture to perpetrate for a moment, to suppose that he would willfully mislead his poor creatures by a proclamation of mercy which meant nothing, or by presenting to them a Christ who could not redeem them. The gospel with God for its witness cannot be false. Whatever may be the witness against it, the witness of God is greater! We must believe the witness of God. ("Faith, and the Witness Upon Which It Is Founded")

Jesus said in John 5:37, "The Father who sent Me has Himself testified about Me." I believe the words of Jesus. I believe the witness of the Father.

We Have the Witness of Our Conversion
1 JOHN 5:10

John now does a very interesting and strategic thing. He ties together our outward confession of Jesus as the Son of God to the inner witness we now have within ourselves. What we confess with our mouth, God makes real in our hearts. Paul said this as well in Romans 10:9-10:

> *If you confess with your mouth, "Jesus is Lord," and believe in your heart that God raised Him from the dead, you will be saved. One believes with the heart, resulting in righteousness, and one confesses with the mouth, resulting in salvation.*

And in Romans 8:16 he adds, "The Spirit Himself testifies together with our spirit that we are God's children."

The internal witness of God's Spirit in the heart confirms to the child of God that he or she was right to believe that Jesus is the Son of God who alone gives the gift of eternal life (1 John 5:11-12). This internal testimony or witness is the personal presence of God in us, and it beautifully balances and complements the external and historical witness of the baptism and crucifixion of Jesus, all witnessed by the Holy Spirit. Plummer well says, "The external witness faithfully accepted becomes internal certitude" (*The Epistles of John*, 162).

In the context of pastoral theology and practical application, this verse is of great value. John does not point us back to a prior experience. He leads us to look now, today, to a present testimony and witness. Whom are you trusting today? Whom are you believing in today? Where is your hope and confidence today? Is it Christ? If so, then rest assured that you have the Son and His gift of eternal life. Not knowing the exact moment you were converted does not mean you are not saved. A past experience can be helpful, but it is present-day testimony that provides the confirmation and assurance that God wants you to enjoy and that your soul longs to have. "I am believing in Christ and only in Christ." You will find that confession to be a blessed avenue of assurance that will cause you to proclaim with passion and conviction, "Jesus is the Son of God."

We Have the Witness of Eternal Life
1 JOHN 5:11-12

John calls his final witness to the stand to testify to the truth that Jesus Christ is the Son of God. This is a fascinating witness. It is the witness of "eternal life." The connection between having the Son and having life is so essential that John will mention "the Son" seven times in verses 9-13 and "life" five times in verses 11-13.

Eternal life is a God-quality, God-kind of life. It has a particular character or essence as well as a never-ending duration. Having Jesus, the Son of God, equals having eternal life. This is God's testimony. This is God's gift ("God has given us eternal life"; 5:11). This life is in His Son, and again it is found in no one else (cf. John 14:6). In fact, to have the Son is to have life. To not have the Son of God means you do not have life. Having the Son of God equals life. Not having the Son of God equals spiritual death. To not have the Son means you are a walking, talking dead man. You are a spiritual corpse in a physical body. James Boice notes:

> John's reference to "eternal life" as the essence of salvation carries us back to the opening verses of the letter, in which he wrote that this life was revealed in Jesus, who is Himself the life. Eternal life is not merely unending life, therefore. It is the very life of God. What we are promised in Christ is a participation in the life of the One who bears this testimony. This life is not to be enjoyed by everyone, however. This life is in Christ. Consequently, it is as impossible to have life without having Christ as it is impossible to have Christ without at the same time possessing eternal life. (*The Epistles of John*, 166)

The Bible teaches that you do not have to *hope* you have eternal life or even *think* you have eternal life. It says you can *know* you have eternal life when you know you have the Son of God, Jesus Christ, as your Savior. This witness, this gift of eternal life, testifies to the eternal Son, for only He who is eternal can give you what is eternal.

Conclusion

I began this study with a quote from my hero from the past, Charles Spurgeon. Let me end with one as well. What is at stake in all of this? If our six superlative witnesses have testified to the truth, then what does all of this mean for you, for me, and for the world? Here it is in sum:

> Let me, first of all, say a word or two about the way in which we are saved, the *modus operandi* of salvation, as we find it described in the Scriptures. Here it is in a nutshell. We have all broken God's Law and we are justly condemned on account of it. God, in infinite mercy, desiring to save the sons of men, has given His Son, Jesus, to stand in the place of as many as believe in Him. Jesus became the Substitute of His people and suffered in their stead, and for them the debt of punishment due to God was paid by Jesus Christ upon the Cross of Calvary. All who believe in Him are, thereby, cleared before the bar of Divine Justice.
>
> Now, the Lord, having given His Son, has revealed this great fact in His Word. Here it is in this Inspired Book—the full statement of it—to this effect, that God was in Christ reconciling the world unto Himself, not imputing their trespasses unto them, and that whoever believes in the Lord Jesus Christ has everlasting life. This is God's testimony! . . . [A]ll we have to do in order to realize the result of Christ's passion is simply to *believe* the testimony of God concerning it and rest upon it!
>
> The argument runs thus—Christ saves those who trust Him. I trust Him and, therefore, I am saved. Jesus Christ suffered for the sins of His people. His people are known by their believing in Him. I believe in Him and, therefore, He died for my sins, and my sins are blotted out. This is the summary of the transaction. God's testimony concerning His Son is at first believed, simply because God says so and for no other reason. And then there grows up in the soul other evidence not necessary to faith, but very strengthening to it— evidence which springs up in the soul as the *result* of faith, and is the witness referred to in our text—"He that believes has the witness in himself." ("The Priest Dispensed With"; emphasis in original)

So I ask, do you believe the testimony of these six superlative witnesses? Do you have this testimony in yourself? "The one who has the Son has life. The one who doesn't have the Son of God does not have life." I plead with you this day: Choose life. Choose Jesus.

Reflect and Discuss

1. Think of someone you know who does not believe in Christ. What are the indications that person wants more evidence? What are the indications of a hard, rebellious heart?
2. How does Jesus' baptism reveal Him as the Son of God? Why did Jesus need to be baptized?
3. Some conclude that since Jesus was crucified, He couldn't have been God's Son. Why does John use the crucifixion as evidence in favor of His divinity?
4. Jesus said the Spirit would be coming to glorify Him. How does the Spirit still work to testify to Jesus? Where should we expect to see the Spirit working?
5. Why is personal testimony of conversion such a powerful witness to Jesus' deity?
6. Why is a person's present testimony of Jesus' lordship just as important or more important than their remembering a past experience?
7. What does it mean for the Son to be eternal life? Where does Jesus claim this for Himself?

Five Truths God Wants Every Child of God to Know

1 JOHN 5:13-21

Main Idea: Christians can rest in the truths that we belong to the God who answers prayer, that we have spiritual victory, and that Christ is the true and only source of eternal life.

I. We Can Know That We Have Eternal Life (5:13).
II. We Can Know That God Answers Prayer (5:14-17).
III. We Can Know Victory over Sin (5:18).
IV. We Can Know That We Belong to God (5:19).
V. We Can Know What Is True (5:20-21).

In a letter to a man named George Ticknor dated November 25, 1817, Thomas Jefferson was critical of state legislatures for not "perceiv[ing] the important truths that knowledge is power, that knowledge is safety, and that knowledge is happiness." One might challenge particulars of Jefferson's statement, but there is a ring of truth in it to be sure. The apostle John certainly thought knowledge was important. He was vitally concerned that his "little children" (v. 21) know a number of things to be true because they had come to believe in Jesus as the Messiah, the Son of God. In fact, a quick survey of this five-chapter letter reveals at least the following things we can know:

1. We can know that we know God (2:3,13,14; 4:7).
2. We can know that we are in God (2:5).
3. We can know that it is the last hour (2:18).
4. We can know the truth (2:21; 3:19).
5. We can know that Jesus is righteous (2:29).
6. We can know that we will be like Jesus (3:2).
7. We can know that Jesus came to take away sins (3:5).
8. We can know that Jesus is sinless (3:5).
9. We can know that we have passed out of death into life (3:14).
10. We can know that no murderer has eternal life (3:15).
11. We can know love (3:16; 4:16).
12. We can know that God abides in us (3:24; 4:13).

13. We can know the Spirit of God (4:2).
14. We can know the Spirit of truth and the spirit of deception (4:6).
15. We can know that we love God's children (5:2).
16. We can know that we have eternal life (5:13).
17. We can know that God answers prayer (5:15).
18. We can know that we will not practice sin (5:18).
19. We can know that we belong to God (5:19).
20. We can know that the Son of God has come (5:20).
21. We can know that the Son of God has given us understanding (5:20).
22. We can know Him who is true (5:20).

It is clear from 1 John alone that the child of God can know and be certain of quite a lot!

In this final section of 1 John (vv. 13-21), things we can know continue to dominate the conversation. Seven times the word "know" appears. Christianity is not an "I hope so" or "I think so" faith. It is an "I know so" faith because what has been revealed in the Bible was given to us by God, a God who speaks and a God who speaks only truth. As John brings his letter to close, what is it, in particular, that God wants every child of His to know?

We Can Know That We Have Eternal Life
1 JOHN 5:13

In a real sense, the entire letter of 1 John has been pointing to this verse. On five prior occasions, John has given his reasons for writing. I like the way John Piper lists and summarizes all six occurrences:

1 John 1:4: "We are writing these things so that our joy may be complete." John is an unashamed Christian Hedonist. The joy of their assurance will be his joy. And he wants it. It is good to want that kind of joy.

1 John 2:1: "My little children, I am writing these things to you so that you may not sin. But if anyone does sin, we have an advocate with the Father, Jesus Christ the righteous." He hopes his book will give them fresh power to overcome sin. And part of his method in helping them overcome sin is to assure them that failures do not have to prove fatal to your eternal life.

1 John 2:12-13: "I am writing to you, little children, because your sins are forgiven for his name's sake. I am writing to you, fathers, because you know him who is from the beginning. I am writing to you, young men, because you have overcome the evil one." In other words, he is filled with hope that the ones he is writing to are truly believers. They are forgiven. They do know God. They have triumphed over the evil one.

1 John 2:21: "I write to you, not because you do not know the truth, but because you know it, and because no lie is of the truth." Same thing: My letter is not to get you started in the Christian life, but to confirm you in it.

1 John 2:26: "I write these things to you about those who are trying to deceive you." He is concerned with false teaching. This letter is meant to protect them from those who would lead them astray. In other words, the fact that we are born again does not mean we no longer need warnings.

1 John 5:13: "I write these things to you who believe in the name of the Son of God that you may know that you have eternal life." This is the one that dominates in this letter. Most of what is here is designed to provide tests of life: "I write these things . . . that you may know that you have eternal life." That is, that you may know you are born again from death to life.

   Summing up all these reasons for writing 1 John goes like this: *I am writing because you are true believers, but there are deceivers in your midst, and I want you to be rock-solid confident in your present possession of eternal life as regenerate children of God, so that you are not drawn away after sin. And if this letter has that effect my joy will be complete.* So at the heart of his reason for writing is the desire to help them know they are born again—that they now have new spiritual life. Eternal life. ("Everyone Who Has Been Born of God")

The apostle John tells us it is possible to have eternal life, the very life of God, and yet have doubts. However, he does not want us to have doubts. He wants us to have assurance. Therefore he provides multiple tests throughout the book ("these things" in verse 13 refers specifically to 5:1-12, but in general the phrase refers to the entire book) revolving around the three themes of belief, obedience, and love. Those who believe Jesus is the Son of God, pursue obedience, and love others can be assured they have eternal life right now. Today! Forever! Don't doubt because of an ignorance of God's Word and His promises. Don't doubt because of a faulty theology (e.g., eternal life is something I can lose or forfeit). Don't doubt because of disobedience. Don't doubt because of hate. Flee to Jesus! He is the Word of life (1:1). He is eternal life (1:2). In this fleeing we must remember: Feelings come and go, and feelings can be deceiving. My confidence is in the Son of God; no one else is worth believing. Jesus said in John 10:28-29,

> *I give them eternal life, and they will never perish—ever! No one will snatch them out of My hand. My Father, who has given them to Me, is greater than all. No one is able to snatch them out of the Father's hand.*

I will take Jesus at His word. I can know I have eternal life.

We Can Know That God Answers Prayer
1 JOHN 5:14-17

With the assurance of eternal life comes another confidence: answered prayer. R. A. Torrey said,

> Prayer is the key that unlocks all the storehouses of God's infinite grace and power. All that God is and all that God has is at the disposal of prayer. But we must use the key. Prayer can do anything that God can do and since God can do anything, prayer is omnipotent. (*The Power of Prayer*, 17)

John addressed prayer in 1 John 3:22. There he informed us that God answers our prayers when we are (1) keeping His commands and (2) doing those things that please Him. John now adds a third requirement: (3) we must ask "according to his will" (v. 14). With these three keys in place, John says we can be confident toward God as we pray. Indeed we can know He hears us as we ask, and we can "know that we have what we have asked Him for" (vv. 14-15).

George Mueller (1805–1898) was a great man of prayer who refused a regular salary and financial support for himself or the ministries he led. A leader of the Christian Brethren movement, Mueller said, "Prayer is not overcoming God's reluctance. It is laying hold of His willingness" (quoted in *Be Real*, 179). Therefore nothing we ask for lies beyond the power of God except that which lies beyond His will, His purpose, His plan.

We might ask why anyone would want something contrary to God's will. It is right to pray according to God's will, and it is wise to pray according to God's will. He knows what is best, and He wants what is best: His glory and our good. God wants to give you what you would want God to give you if you were wise enough to want it.

Now, God's will may be different from what you want, but I believe this: it will always be better than what you want. Romans 12:2 tells us God's will is "good, pleasing, and perfect." I want what God wants for me. I want God's will.

In verses 16 and 17 John gets specific regarding prayer. Verses 14-15 were about petitions. Verses 16-17 are about intercession. The issue is seeing someone in sin. In the original text some form of the word "sin" appears seven times in verses 16-18. Verse 16 is one of the most difficult verses to interpret in all of Scripture. A humble interpretation is right and wise.

First, John addresses a brother who is "sinning a sin" not leading to death. Then he addresses someone whose sin "brings death." The crucial question is this: Is John speaking of physical death or spiritual death? Further, does he have a Christian in view in both instances or is the second situation that of an unbeliever? Again dogmatism is unwarranted in interpreting this verse, but consider the following. John has spiritual death in mind and two different persons in view. Thus his argument is that brothers and sisters in Christ can fall into sin, but their salvation and spiritual death is not at stake because they have Christ as their atonement and advocate and they believe in Him for eternal life. If you see them in sin, don't talk first to others about them, which would be gossip. Talk first to God about them. Pray for their restoration because this is always God's will. Pray to the Lord and He will give life; He will restore the joy and vitality of their salvation since their sins do not and cannot lead to spiritual death. They may be spiritually disciplined, as Hebrews 12:5-13 teaches, but they cannot spiritually die.

Then John addresses a sin that he says leads to death. Interestingly, he does not say the one committing this sin is a brother. Of this sin John says, "I am not saying he should pray about that." Note, he does not command us *not* to pray, but it is clear he is doubtful that it will do any good. Now the question which confronts us is this: "What is the sin that leads to death?" Three main views have been put forward.

1. A specific, deadly sin. This is high-handed sin. It is sin that is willful and deliberate; sin that is of a serious nature. Some, like F. F. Bruce (*Epistles*, 124–5), see the death that results as physical (e.g., Ananias and Sapphira in Acts 5:1-11; the incestuous man at Corinth in 1 Cor 5:5; the Corinthians abusing the Lord's supper in 1 Cor 11:30).

2. Blasphemy against the Holy Spirit (cf. Matt 12:32; Mark 3:29). This is a deliberate, knowledgeable, willful, verbal, and continual rejection of the truth to which the Spirit bears witness. It is a hardening of the heart to a degree that prayer will not help.

3. Total rejection of the gospel and Christ. This is the sin of the false teachers who willfully and habitually oppose the witness of God concerning the person and work of His Son, Jesus Christ (cf. 1 John 2:19). This one is not called a brother. He is an apostate. D. Edmond Hiebert is helpful here:

> These false teachers manifested the spirit of Antichrist, separated themselves from the true church, and perverted or rejected the apostolic message of redemption in Christ. In deliberately rejecting the incarnate Son of God, in whom eternal life is available, they committed themselves to a spiritual attitude and course of action that could only be characterized as "sin unto death." ("An Exposition of 1 John 5:13-21")

If this is correct (and I think this is the best option), John is saying that for those who willfully, resolutely, and irrevocably reject the biblical teaching about Jesus, death—spiritual death—is their destiny. To pray for such a one is futile and useless. It will do no good.

Verse 17 affirms, "all unrighteousness is sin," yet John again states, "There is sin that does not bring death." Such sin can be confronted and even conquered through the faithful intercession of one believer for another. Spurgeon said it well in an address to his Pastors' College regarding the power of prayer:

> Might not we win more victories if we more constantly used this weapon of all-prayer? All hell is vanquished when the believer bows his knee in importunate supplication. Beloved brethren, let us pray. We cannot all argue, but we can all pray; we cannot all be leaders, but we can all be pleaders; we cannot all be mighty in rhetoric, but we can all be prevalent in prayer. I would sooner see you eloquent with God than with men.

Prayer links us with the Eternal, the Omnipotent, the Infinite; and hence it is our chief resort. Resolve to serve the Lord, and to be faithful to His cause, for then you may boldly appeal to Him for succour. Be sure that you are with God, and then you may be sure that God is with you. (*An All-Round Ministry*, 313–14)

We Can Know Victory over Sin

1 JOHN 5:18

For the final time in this letter John addresses the "new birth." The apostle wants us to be sure that we have been born again, and he catalogs no less than 13 evidences of the new birth in this letter.

1. Those who are born of God keep His commands (2:3-4; 3:24).
2. Those who are born of God walk in the same way Christ walked (2:5-6).
3. Those who are born of God are lovers not haters (2:9; 3:14; 4:7-8,20).
4. Those who are born of God love the Father not the world (2:15).
5. Those who are born of God confess the Son and have Him (2:23; 4:15; 5:12).
6. Those who are born of God do what is right (2:29).
7. Those who are born of God do not continually practice sin (3:6,9-10; 5:18).
8. Those who are born of God have the Holy Spirit (3:24; 4:13).
9. Those who are born of God listen to the Word (4:6).
10. Those who are born of God believe Jesus is the Messiah (5:1).
11. Those who are born of God overcome the world (5:4).
12. Those who are born of God believe Jesus is the Son of God (5:4-5).
13. Those who are born of God know that Jesus protects them from the evil one (5:18).

Here in verse 18, John makes three powerful affirmations that assure us once again of our victory over sin. First, we know that the person born of God does not keep on sinning. Sin is no longer the pattern of his or her life. John is affirming the purity of our lives, not perfection, something he addressed in 3:2-3. Future glorification (perfection) impacts present sanctification (practice). Second, "the One who is born of God keeps" or protects him. I like the fact that the HCSB capitalizes "One" because I believe the reference is clearly to Jesus and not us. We do not keep ourselves. Jesus keeps us. This is a theme repeated several times in the New Testament.

> *While I was with them, I was protecting them by Your name that You have given Me. I guarded them and not one of them is lost, except the son of destruction, so that the Scripture may be fulfilled.* (John 17:12)

> *You are being protected by God's power through faith for a salvation that is ready to be revealed in the last time.* (1 Pet 1:5)

> *Now to Him who is able to protect you from stumbling and to make you stand in the presence of His glory, blameless and with great joy.* (Jude 24)

Jesus, by His work on the cross, obtained my salvation. Now, by His work in heaven, He maintains my salvation (cf. Heb 7:25). Jesus Christ, the eternally begotten of God, protects me and keeps me safe. Therefore, and this is our third promise, "the evil one does not touch" me. The word "touch" has the idea of grabbing hold of something with the intent to harm. Alexander Ramsay says, "He is well kept whom Christ keeps; the enemy of souls cannot lay hold of him: he assaults but cannot seize" (quoted in Vaughan, *1,2,3 John*, 134). Satan may grab at us and tempt us through doubt, friends who fall away, idols, fleshly enticements, and worldly allurements, but because of the power of Christ he cannot get us. There again is a beautiful logic to this verse. The Devil does not touch the Christian and harm him in any ultimate sense because he is protected by the Son. And because the Son keeps the believer safe, he cannot persist in or continually practice sin. It is contrary to his nature. It is contrary to his Protector.

Now we know why we have victory over sin and why we have victory over Satan. "The Son of God was revealed for this purpose: to destroy the Devil's works" (1 John 3:8), and He did a perfect job!

We Can Know That We Belong to God
1 JOHN 5:19

In stark contrast to the safety of the believer in Christ, the whole world rests in the power of the evil one. We are safe, but the world is a slave.

Believers in Jesus have a certain and settled knowledge that they are God's. The NIV says, "We know that we are children of God." Eugene Peterson says in *The Message*, "We know that we are held firm by God." Here is confidence, an inner assurance, that spiritual death has no claim on me. Here is a certainty of the soul that sin cannot dominate me and the evil one cannot harm me (v. 18).

> Now I belong to Jesus, Jesus belongs to me;
> Not for the years of time alone, but for eternity. (Norman J. Clayton, "Now I Belong to Jesus")

Tragically, on the other hand, those caught up in the lies and futility of this world-system are controlled and captivated by the power and authority of Satan himself, "the evil one." Satan—who blinds the minds of unbelievers (2 Cor 4:3-4), snatches the Word of God from human hearts (Matt 13:4,9), deceives by miraculous signs and wonders (Matt 24:24; 2 Thess 2:9), and entices through fleshly desires and pride (1 John 2:15-17)—has the entire world in his pocket. This is instructive for those of us who follow Christ. We are in a global conflict with an enemy that influences and in many instances controls cultures, societies, finances, and even governments. This "evil empire" under "the sway of the evil one" opposes with vehemence the advancement of the gospel, ministries of mercy, and care for the weak and helpless. He hates who we are and what we are trying to accomplish. This requires on our part a wartime mentality and commitment. Sacrifices must be made, and strategies bathed in spiritual wisdom must be created and implemented. But know this: As we move forward, we are children of God, a God who is in us and who is greater than he who is in the world. (4:4). We are His and He will protect us (5:18).

We Can Know What Is True
1 JOHN 5:20-21

Not surprisingly, John ends the letter as he began it: talking about Jesus! He affirms again the reality of the incarnation ("we know the Son of God has come"). He also affirms that it is Jesus who gives us understanding so that we may know Him who is true (God Himself) in and through Jesus Christ. These words echo Luke 10:22 where Jesus said, "No one knows who the Son is except the Father, and who the Father is except the Son, and anyone to whom the Son desires to reveal Him."

Because of our union with Christ, we understand the truth of the gospel, we are safe from the claws of the evil one, we know the Father, and we abide "in the true One—that is, in His Son Jesus Christ." Of Christ it can be said, "He is the true God and eternal life." Here is truth. Here is life. Here is knowledge and understanding. All of this is ours by virtue of our union with Christ, because "we are in the true One."

However, if there is a true God, there are also false gods. Therefore John provides a simple but perfect complement to verse 20 and a perfect conclusion to the letter in verse 21. "Little children," he says, "guard yourselves from idols." Be on guard, John says, from god-substitutes. Paul gives us similar warnings in Ephesians 5:5 ("For know and recognize this: Every sexually immoral or impure or greedy person, who is an idolater, does not have an inheritance in the kingdom of the Messiah and of God.") and in Colossians 3:5 ("Therefore, put to death what belongs to your worldly nature: sexual immorality, impurity, lust, evil desire, and greed, which is idolatry."). John, letting his letter be our guide, would say,

> Those who claim to be Christians but do not believe the truth concerning Jesus, do not live a righteous life in obeying God's commands, and do not love others are in danger of idol worship. This is an idol because they have created a religion that is false. This is a religion that man has created and not that of the apostolic faith. This is nothing short of idolatry. To embrace a form of Christianity that allows one to deny the truth about Jesus, not live a godly life, or not love others, is to create an idol—and that is something all Christians must constantly guard against. (Merkle, "What Is the Meaning of 'Idols'?," 340)

John Calvin said, "Man's nature . . . is a perpetual factory of idols" (*Institutes*, 1.11.8). Mark Driscoll says idolatry is the opposite of the gospel (Driscoll and Breshears, *Death by Love*, 92). Amazingly, the object of idolatry can be a good thing. However, when we turn a good thing into a god thing it becomes a bad thing: an idol. Tim Keller helps us see how idolatry is sin when he says, "The ultimate reason for any sin is that something besides Christ is functioning as an alternative 'righteousness' or source of confidence—and is thus an 'idol,' a pseudo-savior, which creates inordinate desires" ("Preaching the Gospel in a Post-Modern World"). Luther's "Preface to the Galatians" is equally helpful:

Satan attacked this rock (the doctrine of justification) in
paradise when he persuaded our first parents to forsake their
faith in the God who had given them life and who promised
enduring life, and to try to become like God by means of
their own wisdom and virtue (Gen. 3:5). . . . For thereafter the
whole world went mad in opposition to this faith, inventing
endless idols and religions, by which, as Paul says (Acts 14:16),
everyone went his own way, in the hope of placating a god
or a goddess or gods or goddesses by his own works, in other
words, of redeeming himself from evil and sin by means of
his own work, without the help of Christ. The acts and books
of all the heathen provide plenty of evidence for all of this.
("Preface to Galatians," 145–46)

Also, note Luther's *Treatise on Good Works*:

Those who do not trust God at all times and do not see God's
favor and grace and good will toward them in everything they
do and everything they suffer, in their living or in their dying,
but seek His favor in other things or even in themselves, do
not keep this [First] Commandment [to have no other gods
before Him]. Rather, they practice idolatry, even if they were
to do the works of all the rest of the Commandments. (*Treatise
on Good Works*, 30–31)

Any effort to earn our own salvation creates idols of necessity. For if
we make our career or our morality or our marriage our fundamental
"confidence" in life—our "wisdom" and "power"—then those things
become idols which we look to instead of Christ for our "salvation."
Thus, those keeping the other nine commandments as a way to earn
their own salvation are really breaking the first commandment by and in
their morality! Their good works are therefore all done in service to an
idol as a way of avoiding Christ as Savior (Keller, "Talking about Idolatry
in a Postmodern Age").

In sum, idolatry is anything you love, enjoy, and pursue more than
God, more than Christ, who "is the true God and eternal life." Idols say
we are true when God says only Christ is true. Idols say they will give life
when God says only Christ provides life, eternal life. Idols promise but
can never deliver, whereas God says Christ both provides and delivers.
So guard yourself from idols of power, control, comfort, approval,
position, applause, and pleasure. Your heart will never be satisfied and

at rest with any of these little false gods. Only Christ truly and eternally satisfies. Jesus said it perfectly: "Whoever drinks from the water that I will give him will never get thirsty again —ever! In fact, the water I will give him will become a well of water springing up within him for eternal life" (John 4:14).

Conclusion

Jesus Christ is the Son of God, the true God, and the only God who gives you an eternal life—and you can have it with certainty. All you have to do is believe in His name. He and He alone is the "true God." All other gods are deceiving counterfeits and false substitutes. What they promise they can never provide. Jesus "is the true God and eternal life." On this truth you can stand and stake your eternal destiny.

Reflect and Discuss

1. Why would God want us to know certain truths as we live the Christian life? How do these truths comfort us?
2. From the list at the beginning of this chapter, which truths are the most clear examples of grace to you? Which are hardest for you to believe?
3. How do you feel about Christians having doubts? How should we respond when doubts arise in our hearts?
4. What role does prayer play in assurance? Should we pray even when we are struggling with doubt?
5. Why can John say that we have everything we ask for? How can this verse be abused?
6. How do you respond when you see a brother or sister living in sin?
7. Look at the 13 evidences of the new birth from 1 John. Which of these are you displaying? Which are you failing to display?
8. How can believers have victory over sin if they still commit sin?
9. What might be the effect of realizing that the whole world is under the sway of the evil one? How does that change the way you view others?
10. In what way is 1 John 5:21 a summary of the entire book? Why is idolatry an issue still today, even in secular cultures?

Truth or Consequences:
What You Believe about Jesus Really Matters

2 JOHN 1-13

Main Idea: Followers of Jesus must walk in His commands as they love the truth of His teaching.

I. **We Must Love the Truth (1-3).**
   A. Embrace the truth (1-2).
   B. Enjoy the truth (3).
II. **We Must Live the Truth (4-6).**
   A. Be concerned with what you believe (creed) (4).
   B. Be concerned with how you behave (conduct) (5-6).
III. **We Must Look for the Truth (7-11).**
   A. Recognize the deceptive (7).
   B. Resist the destructive (8).
   C. Reprove the destitute (9).
   D. Reject the dangerous (10-11).
IV. **We Must Long for the Truth (12-13).**
   A. Experience the fullness of joy (12).
   B. Experience the fellowship of the family (13).

When Jesus was in the "upper room" with His disciples the night before His crucifixion, He made a number of profound and lasting statements. One concerned truth; another concerned love. John 14:6 reports that He said, "I am the way, the truth, and the life. No one comes to the Father except through Me." And John 13:35 records, "By this all people will know that you are My disciples, if you have love for one another." Truth and love are the twin rails on which Christianity runs. They bring authenticity and balance to our Christian confession and conduct. Yet both are endangered species, especially in a postmodern twenty-first-century world where relativism and sentimentalism reign. Blaise Pascal (1623–62), the brilliant Christian philosopher and mathematician, well said of his own day, "Truth is so obscure in these times, and falsehood so established, that unless we love the truth, we cannot know it" (*Pensees*, 14:863). The apostle Paul echoed this same concern in 2 Thessalonians 2:10 when he wrote of those deceived by "the lawless one" (i.e., "the Antichrist"), "They perish because they did not accept the love of the truth in order to be saved." The apostle John was so concerned about the issue that he penned an entire letter to address the problem. We call it 2 John.

Second John is a tiny and much-neglected epistle filled with wisdom and insight. It addresses both the heart and the mind, both love and truth. Despite being so short, it is striking in its comprehensiveness. The letter, though anonymous, was almost certainly penned by the apostle John. It is 245 words in Greek, making it the second shortest book in the Bible (3 John is 219 Greek words). It was written, most likely, from Ephesus between AD 80 and 95. The early church historian Eusebius suggests that it and its twin sister, 3 John, were written after John was released from the Island of Patmos where he had been exiled and where he wrote the book of Revelation. If this is correct, 2 and 3 John are the last New Testament books to be written. John is short and to the point in this letter, and provides several words of encouragement and instruction for those who care for truth and love. It is no surprise that both themes are tied to the gospel, particularly to the person of Jesus Christ.

Several key themes and contrasts weave this short epistle into a beautiful tapestry of spiritual significance. First, there are the key words and their repetition. The word "truth" occurs five times in verses 1-4; the word "love" occurs four times in verses 1-6; the word "command" occurs four times in verses 4-6; the word "walk," which addresses one's entire lifestyle and behavior, occurs three times in verses 4-6; and the word "teaching" occurs three times in verses 9-10. Second, the letter is linked by three commands: the command to continue to love each other as the Lord had said from the beginning (vv. 5-6), the command to be on the lookout for false teachers (v. 8), and the command to reject false teachers (v. 10). Third, there are several contrasts that tie the epistle together: (1) those who walk in truth (v. 4a) versus those who deny the truth (v. 7); (2) the command from the beginning (vv. 5-6) versus those who go beyond (v. 9); (3) deeds worthy of a full reward (v. 8) versus evil works (v. 11); and (4) those who reject antichrist (v. 10) versus those who receive antichrist (v. 11). Second John's major point appears to be that we must walk in the commands of Christ as we love the truth of His teaching.

John drives home several important ideas concerning truth in verses 1-2. Love is to be expressed in the context of truth (cf. Eph 4:15). Truth can be known as an objective reality ("know" in verse 1 is in the perfect tense). Truth can be embraced experientially ("in us") and continually ("remains"). Truth is eternal. It has its source in God (cf. 1 John 5:20). Though truth is not really defined in this letter, it seems clear that John uses the word theologically and practically, not philosophically. He has in mind the truth of the gospel of Jesus Christ as God's self-revelation in the incarnation (John 1:14). John's purpose is not to denigrate whatever truths we glean from reason, experience, or tradition. It is the case, however, that John's epistemological foundation is rooted in Christ and the teachings and testimony of the apostles to that historical manifestation. God has revealed His truth supremely in Christ.

We Must Love the Truth
2 JOHN 1-3

The author of this short letter is simply identified as "the Elder" (Gk *presbuteros*), an introduction unique to 2 and 3 John. It emphasizes the position and personal relationship he has with the recipients of the letter. The title "elder" carries the idea of an aged man, but also a man who has earned authority and respect by virtue of his experience, character, integrity, moral standing, and reputation.

The recipient is also simply identified as "the elect [chosen] lady and her children." This may refer to either a local church and its members (the best view), the church universal, or an individual lady and her children. *Elect lady* is a term of respect, endearment, privilege, and protection. God chose this community of faith as His very own. They belong to Him and He cares for them personally and individually. Now, what word does the Lord have for this people near and dear to His heart?

Embrace the Truth (2 John 1-2)

John's statement, "I love all of you in the truth," is emphatic (i.e., "I, myself, love . . ."). He truly loves them. "Love" also is a present tense verb denoting continuous action. Love and truth, as we noted earlier, dominate this letter in verses 1-6 by virtue of the number of times each word occurs. John expresses his love for this local body of believers in the context of truth, a love that is grounded in truth and shared by all who know the truth. Further, this truth abides or remains continually both in us and with us forever.

The Christian philosopher Arthur Holmes has reminded us that "all truth is God's truth wherever it is found" (*All Truth Is God's Truth*). Truth in the biblical sense is essential not optional, eternal not relative, consistent not changing, and permanent not perspectival. Flowing from the One who is "the way, the truth, and the life" (John 14:6), who is Himself "the true God and eternal life" (1 John 5:20), this truth must be embraced as our very own. Indeed, we must have a consuming passion for this truth, truth that is bathed in love.

Enjoy the Truth (2 John 3)

Truth has wonderful companions who accompany it. Truth also has a definite and exclusive source from which it originates. Truth's companions are threefold in our text. They are grace, mercy, and peace. Grace is God doing *for us* what we do not deserve (unmerited favor and divine kindness). Mercy is God not doing *to us* what we do deserve (God's compassion, pity, and tenderness). Peace is personal wholeness and well-being in all aspects of life. Regarding this peace, Romans 5:1 reminds us, "Therefore, since we have been declared righteous by faith, we have peace with God through our Lord Jesus Christ." And Philippians 4:9 says, "Do what you have learned and received and heard and seen in me, and the God of peace will be with you."

These three Christian virtues have a very specific and distinct source, as do love and truth. Grace, mercy, peace, truth, and love all flow into our lives "from God the Father and from Jesus Christ, the Son of the Father" (cf. 1 John 1:3). The repetition of the preposition "from" is significant. It conveys the idea of equality of position while maintaining distinction in person. The Father and Son are equally and fully God, yet there is a true and genuine distinction in person. To make this clear, God is identified as Father twice. In terms of the inner relationship within the Godhead, Jesus Christ is God, but He is also God the Father's Son. He is the anointed Messiah, the Christ, sent by the Father into this world for the purpose of redeeming sinful humanity. All of this, again, occurs within the context of truth and love. John was well aware of the fact that "To maintain a healthy and growing community the church must exhibit a fidelity to the truth that knows no compromise, and they must love one another in a way that knows no boundaries" (Akin, *1, 2, 3 John*, 223).

We Must Live the Truth
2 JOHN 4-6

Vance Havner (1901–1986) was a wonderful North Carolina evangelist and preacher. He was also a reservoir of wisdom and wit. He often said, "What we live is what we really believe. Everything else is just so much religious talk!" Wow! Ouch! Jonathan Edwards (1703–1758) said it this way: "The informing of the understanding is all vain, any farther than it *affects* the heart, or, which is the same thing, has influence on the *affections*" (*Some Thoughts*, 367; emphasis in original). The apostle John agreed. He was convinced that unless truth reaches and affects the heart, the inner man, it is of no real value, regardless of what it may do in the head. Truth should grab hold of head, heart, and hands.

Be Concerned with What You Believe (Creed) (2 John 4)

John extends words of both joy and encouragement. He "was very glad to find some of your children walking in the truth." This was "in keeping with a command we have received from the Father." Verse 5 informs us that this command is "that we love one another." Moreover, when John talks about truth, he is not interested in philosophy. He focuses on the gospel and the transformed life it makes possible. He is interested in a right understanding of the incarnation (v. 7). He is concerned that we "remain in Christ's teachings" (v. 9). He focuses on that truth of the gospel that extends "grace, mercy, and peace" (v. 3) to all who come to God as Father by way of the Son, Jesus Christ.

John knew well the source of His spiritual authority, of his life's authority. Tragically many today do not. As a result we are awash in spiritual, moral, and religious confusion. There are basically four options when it comes to the source of the authority to which we will submit. We will either submit to *reason* (what we think), *tradition* (what we've always done), *experience* (what we feel), or *revelation* (what God says). For John, God had revealed Himself in Jesus Christ His Son and in His Word. The matter was settled. We don't debate Him or the Word. We proclaim both.

Be Concerned with How You Behave (Conduct) (2 John 5-6)

Wrong thinking inevitably leads to wrong living. If the mind is confused, the heart will be corrupted. Right thinking, however, is the right soil from which emerges the fruit of right living. For John, right living is a life of love that is the supernatural response to the love one experiences in the gospel of Jesus Christ.

Next, John urges this local body of believers in Jesus (called "dear lady") to "love one another." He says it is not a new command, "but one we have had from the beginning," that is, the beginning of their Christian experience, and a command given directly to John by Jesus (John 13:34-35). False teachers may have a new, an additional, word for this elect lady and her children (v. 1), this dear lady (v. 5), but John simply reminds them of an old word. What they heard from the beginning should stay with them to the end.

In verse 6 John tells them to demonstrate their love for God not only by loving one another (v. 5), but by walking "according to His commands." This is something they also heard from the beginning: "you must walk in love." Verses 4-6 are so simple; they are almost poetic. Walk in the command to love, and love the commands in which you walk. Truth is something we believe. Truth is also something we live.

We Must Look for the Truth
2 JOHN 7-11

The church father Augustine (AD 354–430) well said of our God, "You have made us for Yourself, and our hearts are restless until they find their rest in Thee" (*Confessions*, 1). Augustine adds further, "Therefore hold fast love, and set your minds at rest" (*Homilies*, 10.7), and you are to "love God with all thy heart, and with all thy soul, and with all thy mind . . . concentrate all your thoughts, your whole life, and your whole intelligence upon Him from whom you derive all that you bring" (*On Christine Doctrine*, 1.22). The only hope humanity has for peace and rest is in wholehearted devotion to the pursuit of truth in God.

My friend Al Mohler says, "Where truth is denied, only therapy remains." The apostle John might add, "Where truth is adjusted, heresy will reign." John was confronted with the spiritual, mystical theology of his day, an early form of Gnosticism. Gnosticism—the term is based on the Greek word for "knowledge"—took many forms as it developed, but most forms usually held two main propositions in common: (1) salvation is by (mystical) knowledge, and (2) the material world is evil or inferior to the spiritual. As a result of their worldview, they attacked the reality of the incarnation. Similarly, the Docetists (from the Greek word meaning "to appear") said Jesus only appeared to be human or have a physical

body. Another form of the heresy led by Cerinthus said the Christ-spirit
came on the man Jesus at His baptism but left Him at the cross.

John knew that Christology is the heart of Christianity. If you are
wrong on who Christ is, you will be wrong everywhere. John therefore
issued a strong warning to be on the lookout for anyone who challenged
the full deity, true and perfect humanity, sinless life, and completed
work of Jesus Christ, the Son of the Father.

Recognize the Deceptive (2 John 7)

Verse 7 is closely connected to verse 6. We must walk in the truth because
"many deceivers" have gone out to evangelize in the evil world system.
These spiritual defectors are Satan's missionaries on assignment. Their
message is that Jesus is not the Messiah, the Son of God coming in the
flesh. Their message is a denial of the true gospel, attacking the factual-
ity of the incarnation and the genuine uniting of deity and humanity in
the person of Jesus.

The heart of all false teaching will be a defective view of Jesus. It will
distort who He is and what He has done. Such teaching will, without
exception, deny His full deity and reject His perfect work of atonement
through His crucifixion and resurrection. Take as an example the
"Jesus Seminar," which in 1998 released the book *The Acts of Jesus* and
arrogantly proclaimed that the resurrection of Jesus did not involve
the resuscitation of a corpse, that belief in Jesus' resurrection did not
depend on what happened to His body, that the body of Jesus decayed
like all other corpses, and that the resurrection was not an event that
happened on the first Easter Sunday. They explained that it was not an
event that could have been recorded by a video camera. In addition,
they assured us it is not necessary to believe in the historical veracity of
the resurrection narratives.

To such opinions John fires back, "This is the deceiver and the
antichrist." The word "antichrist" means "against" or "in the place of"
Christ. Here "against" is clearly the meaning. The word itself occurs only
in 1 John 2:18,22; 4:3 and here in 2 John 7. While interest in this sinister
figure's coming is as popular as ever, John informs us that his minions
are here and have been here since the first century. New Testament
scholar I. Howard Marshall puts this teaching in perspective when he
notes,

> Apocalyptic thought prophesied the coming of a supremely
> evil antagonist of God in the last days—the lawless one

(2 Thess. 2:1-12) or the beast (Rev. 13). [Actually, there are
two beasts in Revelation 13, the first in verses 1-10 from the
sea, usually identified with the antichrist both personally and
politically, and the second in verses 11-18 from the land, being
identified with the false prophet (cf. Rev 19:20).] This figure
is certainly opposed to Christ and attempts to emulate his
powers. . . . The elder's point is that the spirit of opposition to
Christ is already present in those who oppose the truth about
Christ. (*The Epistles of John*, note 9)

[Antichrist] is used to characterize people who are radically
opposed to the true doctrine about Christ and are thus
supremely his opponents, even if they protest that they hold
the truth about him and are Christians. The elder says that
anybody who denies the truth is a very antichrist, just as we
might speak of a supremely evil person as "the very devil." (*The
Epistles of John*, 71)

The deceivers, John says, are many and their message is destructive.
Look and listen carefully, for their true colors are revealed in what they
say and in the One they oppose: they are enemies of the truth about
Jesus.

Resist the Destructive (2 John 8)

"Watch yourselves" is a present tense imperative. It means to continually
be on guard. It is intended to come across as a strong warning. John
implores his readers to not be lulled into a spiritual stupor. Why? Their
"full reward" is at stake. What does this mean? One option is the possible loss of salvation. The other is the loss of some reward. The latter
seems more likely, given the context and that it is a "full reward" that is
mentioned. While the exact meaning of the reward is unclear, what we
do know is this: John believes perseverance is the proof of possession
(cf. 1 John 2:19). As Vance Havner said, "Faith that fizzles before the
finish was faulty from the first."

There is a theological tension here we must understand. For those
who have been born from above by the Spirit of God through faith
in Christ, it is certain that you will persevere. It is also essential that
you do persevere. Day in and day out, we must be on guard and resist
destructive persons and philosophies that deny the truth about Jesus
and that would take from us our full reward. Such spiritual destroyers

will deny the complete truthfulness and sufficiency of the Bible. They will deny the person and work of Jesus Christ—His full deity and/or perfect humanity; His work of atonement on the cross as the perfect sacrifice and satisfaction for our sin. They will deny His sinless life, virgin birth, bodily resurrection, and future return in glory. They will deny that salvation is a free gift received by grace alone through faith alone in Christ alone. And they will deny Jesus as the only Lord and Savior of mankind. Knowing these things, we must recognize the deceptive and resist the destructive.

Reprove the Destitute (2 John 9)

Anyone who does not remain in Christ's teaching but goes beyond it offers what I call a "Bible plus" doctrine and a "Jesus plus" theology. They leave the basic, biblical truths about Jesus and claim to offer something new and something better. John's judgment on such persons is quick and to the point: they are lost. That person "does not have God." John is clear. There is no ambiguity. When you take Jesus as your Savior, you get God as your Father. But if you say "No" to Jesus, you are also saying "No" to the Father who sent Him. The two always go together. They are one and they cannot be separated. Only one road leads to the living and true God. That road, that way, is Jesus.

What does the theology of the destitute look like? You only need to look at the thousands of cults and the liberal theologies and modern ideologies of our day and you have a fairly accurate picture. Yet they are not as complex as they appear. All deceivers, all false teachers, practice a very similar "spiritual mathematical strategy" (Walker, personal correspondence).

The Mathematics of the Cults

Addition (+)	They add an extra-biblical source of authority by prophet, pen, or professor.
Subtraction (−)	They subtract from the person and work of Jesus Christ the Son of God. They deny His deity and find inadequate His work of redemption.
Division (÷)	They divide our allegiance from God through Christ alone to others.
Multiplication (×)	They multiply requirements for salvation. All advocate some form of works salvation.

These four simple principles will enable us to spot and expose those spiritual movements that, regardless of their profession, do not know or have God.

Reject the Dangerous (2 John 10-11)

John's use of "anyone" here is comprehensive. And the "teaching" John referred to is our doctrine, what we believe and confess concerning the gospel and the person and work of Jesus. John commanded his readers to "not receive" a false teacher. We are not to give them a base of operation from our home, nor are we to "welcome" them as friends and fellow laborers for the truth of the gospel. To do so is to "share in his evil works."

What was John saying? He was instructing them to not provide support and assistance to these false teachers. Do not help them along in their evil assignment because if you do, you go with them (cf. 3 John 8). John was not unloving or unkind. He was being both pastoral and practical. We cannot pray God's blessing on those who deny our Lord and reject the teachings of God's Word.

What is John not saying? He is not saying that we cannot allow them in our home for a visit whereby we share the gospel of Jesus with them. Indeed, we most certainly ought to be doing this. You might say, "I can't; I'm not equipped." This is a common fear, but here is a simple and sure strategy that anyone can use who truly knows Jesus as Lord and Savior as they witness to someone involved in false teaching. There are a few principles to remember. First, always be kind. Second, be a good listener. Third, pray for them. And fourth, love them. These will guide you as you share truth in love.

Here also is a general procedure to follow. Give them 15 minutes uninterrupted in which they can tell you what they believe you must do to be saved and go to heaven when you die. Then, ask them to give you 15 minutes uninterrupted so that you can tell them how you believe a person can be saved and go to heaven when they die. Then pray with them, praying evangelistically so as to share clearly and completely the gospel in your prayer. Afterwards, invite them (and their friends) back to do it again!

We Must Long for the Truth
2 JOHN 12-13

John has shared his heart but there is much more that he wants to say. Paper and pen have been sufficient for the immediate situation, but they are a poor substitute for a face-to-face meeting. In closing, John reminds all of us of two precious truths never to be taken for granted.

Experience the Fullness of Joy (2 John 12)

"Face to face" is a beautiful Greek idiom, which is literally "mouth to mouth." When believers who love the Lord Jesus and each other come together, there is indeed a fullness of joy (cf. 1 John 1:4) that words on paper cannot express. John loves this people and they love him. Their coming reunion was something all looked forward to. It could not happen soon enough.

Experience the Fellowship of the Family (2 John 13)

The letter closes with a greeting either from the elect lady's sister or more probably a sister church. They stand with John in what he has said. Indeed, the truth about Jesus brings together brothers and sisters from every tribe, language, people, and nation (Rev 5:9; 7:9). We are one big family with the same Father, Savior, and Spirit. Nothing should tear down the walls of sinful bigotry and prejudice like the gospel of Jesus. Love and truth flow freely from Him to us all. Love and truth should flow freely from all of us to one another.

Conclusion

I was on an airplane some years ago when I looked over and saw a woman reading the *Varieties of Religious Experience: A Study in Human Nature* (1902) by William James (1842–1910), the American psychologist and philosopher. Being prompted, I believe, of the Lord, I sought to engage her in conversation and so I commented on the book, pointing out that there were things in it with which I agreed, but also there were things in it with which I strongly disagreed. She very graciously responded that she had never read anything or met anyone with whom she completely agreed. I responded and told her I had only met one. She asked "Who?" I told her, "His name is Jesus." From there we engaged in a calm but intense dialogue for almost an hour. As the conversation moved toward closure, I told her that the bottom line, the crucial issue of history, is Jesus and His resurrection. If the resurrection is true, it does follow logically and quite clearly that (1) there is a God, (2) Jesus is that God, (3) all of humanity needs to know this God, and (4) this Jesus and the message about Him is the focal point of all history, all knowledge, and all life.

Ravi Zacharias says that former television talk show host Larry King was once asked who he would like to interview from history. One of the persons he named was Jesus. When questioned as to what he would ask Jesus, Larry King said, "I would like to ask Him if He was indeed virgin born, because the answer to that question would define history" (*Can Man Live Without God*, xviii). I believe Larry King is right. When the virgin birth is wedded to His resurrection, Jesus of Nazareth, the eternal Son of God, does define history. He also defines eternity.

We must love this truth. We must live this truth. After all, it is Jesus who said, "You will know the truth, and the truth will set you free" (John 8:32).

Reflect and Discuss

1. Why does truth matter to Christianity? Why is it impossible for the truth about Jesus to be relative?
2. What other passages of Scripture reinforce the truth as central to biblical faith?
3. How are grace, mercy, peace, truth, and love related? How do these connections help you as you live out the Christian life?
4. Why must truth be lived rather than simply believed? Does failing to live out a belief mean it isn't true?
5. Why does John identify love with obedience to God's commands in this passage? What does that teach us about love?
6. What is significant about the incarnation of Jesus being at the center of the heresy John is combating? Why is the incarnation so scandalous? Why is it so important?
7. Why is going beyond the Word of God so dangerous? How has this strategy been used to lead people astray?
8. What is the "full reward" that John refers to, and how can believers pursue and preserve it?
9. Looking at the chart "The Mathematics of the Cults" on page 159, give examples of each of these errors. How can we be on guard against them all at the same time?
10. Why does the body of Christ bring such joy to John? When have you experienced fellowship like that?

Does Your Life Bring Praise to the Name of Jesus?
Four Men and Their Reputations

3 JOHN 1-14

Main Idea: As followers of Jesus, our lives and reputations ought to reflect His love, affection, and hospitality toward one another.

I. **Gaius: A Man with the Right Balance (1-8).**
   A. Live spiritually (1-2).
   B. Walk truthfully (3-4).
   C. Serve faithfully (5-6).
   D. Minister generously (7-8).
II. **Diotrephes: A Man with a Harmful Agenda (9-10).**
   A. Do not be driven by prideful ambition (9).
   B. Do not display pompous arrogance (9).
   C. Do not deliver perverse accusations (10).
   D. Do not dominate with profane activity (10).
III. **Demetrius: A Man with a Good Testimony (11-12).**
   A. Pursue a godly example (11).
   B. Possess a good testimony (12).
IV. **John: A Man with a Pastor's Heart (13-14).**
   A. Desire the presence of fellow believers (13).
   B. Desire peace for fellow believers (14).

All of us share an invaluable possession. It goes with us wherever we go, but amazingly, it also goes where we do not go. Furthermore, what you think of this prized possession is not necessarily what others think of it. I speak of our reputation. Your reputation is the estimation or evaluation others have of your character, integrity, and standing as a person. It may be good or bad, positive or negative. But be assured of this: We all have a reputation. People *will* watch you and talk about you. (Count on it!) You cannot escape or lose your reputation. It precedes you, goes with you, and follows you all of your life and beyond.

Charles Spurgeon knew the importance of a reputation, especially for the Christian:

The eagle-eyed world acts as a policeman for the church. . . .
[It] becomes a watch-dog over the sheep, barking furiously as
soon as one goes astray. . . .
    Be careful, be careful of your private lives . . . and I believe
your public lives will be sure to be right. Remember that it
is upon your *public* life that the verdict of the world will very
much depend. ("The Parent's and Pastor's Joy")

With that in mind let me raise three important questions for all of
us to think about: First, what do you think of yourself? Second, what do
you believe others think about you? Third, what does God think about
you? The shortest book in the Bible, the letter of 3 John is very helpful
in assisting us to reflect on these three questions. Just over 200 words,
this postcard epistle has been too often neglected to the detriment of
the church. Like 1 & 2 Timothy, Titus, and Philemon, it is written to an
individual, a man named Gaius. Written by John between AD 80 and 95,
Eusebius, the ancient church historian, says it was penned after John was
released from the rock quarry island of Patmos in the Aegean Sea. If this is
correct, 3 John may have been the last book written in the New Testament.

The book is similar in length and style to its twin, 2 John, yet there
are some important differences as well. Third John revolves around
four key men and their reputations, whereas 2 John mentions no one
by name. In 2 John the problem was showing hospitality to the wrong
visitors. In 3 John the problem is not showing hospitality to the right
visitors. In 2 John the major concern was truth. In 3 John the major
concern is love.

It is easy to outline the book biographically around the four men of
the letter. As we look at each one of them, continue to examine yourself
and see if anyone here looks something like you. Ask yourself a very
important question: Does my life bring praise to the name of Jesus? Do
I live out Matthew 5:16?

*In the same way, let your light shine before men, so that they may see
your good works and give glory to your Father in heaven.*

Gaius: A Man with the Right Balance
3 JOHN 1-8

This letter begins in the same way as 2 John, identifying the author as
"the Elder" *(Gk presbuteros)*. The word originally meant an older man but

came to convey ideas of respect, authenticity, and integrity. An elder is a man of courage, commitment, and conviction. He is a man of authority rooted in his spiritual maturity. John was such a man, and because he had a tender relationship with "the elect lady" (2 John) and Gaius (3 John), there was no need to assert his apostleship. John commends Gaius in four areas of his life. These are areas in which we also should seek to excel, having come into a saving relationship with Christ.

Live Spiritually (3 John 1-2)

Four times John will address Gaius, the recipient of this letter, as "dear friend." It expresses deep, heartfelt love for this man. John loved this man and he told him. He also knew his spiritual life was in good health, and he told him this as well.

Gaius was a common name in that day, and several men by that name appear in the New Testament: Gaius of Corinth (Rom 16:23), Macedonia (Acts 19:29), and Derbe (Acts 20:4). Gaius of 3 John is probably none of those. All we know of this Gaius we learn from this short letter, and what we learn is outstanding.

John's love for Gaius is genuine; it is accompanied by truth (used seven times). There is nothing false or superficial here. He loves this man truly. The "I" in verse 1 is emphatic: "I [myself] love you in the truth." John is praying (continually) for Gaius to prosper (continually) in every way (a phrase that is fronted in the Greek to add emphasis) and to be "in good health physically just as you are spiritually" (v. 2). "Prosper" conveys the idea of having a good journey. His prayer for "health" is similar to our idea of hygiene. Gaius had a clean bill of health spiritually. Perhaps he was suffering some physical difficulty, but his soul was "ship shape," in top condition.

A good point of application naturally arises from this prayer. What if I were to pray for you and ask God to bless you physically to the same degree you are healthy spiritually, and what if He answered my prayer? What would happen?! Would you be fit, sick in bed, or nearly dead? Would we need to rush you to the emergency room and have you ushered into the ICU or CCU? Gaius was "soul healthy." The life of Christ was vibrant and alive in Him. That same life is ours as we enjoy the blessings and benefits we have in Christ.

Walk Truthfully (3 John 3-4)

Living spiritually is intimately connected to walking truthfully. John could be "very glad" (v. 3) and "have no greater joy" (v. 4) because of what others were telling him about Gaius. The truth was in him, and he lived what he believed. In doctrine and deed, Gaius was commendable, praiseworthy, and a joy to his brothers and sisters in Christ. There was no contradiction between his profession (talk) and practice (walk). "My children" may indicate that John had led Gaius to Christ. John was fathering spiritual children into the kingdom of God, and Gaius was a child of his in whom he took great delight. Spurgeon knew the importance of this calling for every child of God, but especially those called to the ministry:

> You may view, dear Friends, the text as specifying the
> PASTOR'S greatest reward. "I have no greater joy than to
> hear that my children walk in the Truth of God." The minister
> who is sent of God has *spiritual* children. They are as much
> his children as if they had literally been born in his house,
> for to their immortal Nature he stands under God in the
> relationship of father. . . .
> No minister ought to be at rest unless he sees that his
> ministry brings forth fruit, and men and women are born unto
> God by the preaching of the Word.
> To this end we are sent to you, not to help you to spend
> your Sundays respectably, nor to quiet your conscience by
> conducting worship on your behalf. No, Sirs, ministers are
> sent into the world for a higher purpose! And if your souls are
> not saved, we have labored in vain as far as you are concerned.
> If in the hands of God we are not made the means of your new
> birth, our sermons and instructions have been a mere waste of
> effort and your hearing has been a mere waste of time to you,
> if not something worse. To see children born unto God—that
> is the grand thing! Therefore every preacher longs to be able
> to talk about his spiritual sons and daughters. ("The Parent's
> and Pastor's Joy"; emphasis in original)

However, Spurgeon was not satisfied to challenge ministers only in light of this text. He also walked into the home and looked parents straight in the eyes, challenging them in their failure to make spiritual children in their own families.

It is very grievous to see how some professedly Christian
parents are satisfied so long as their children display cleverness
in learning, or sharpness in business, although they show no
signs of a renewed Nature. If they pass their examinations
with credit and promise to be well-fitted for the *world's* battle,
their parents forget that there is a superior calling, involving
a higher crown, for which the child will need to be fitted by
Divine Grace and armed with the whole armor of God. . . .
    Many who ought to know better think themselves
superlatively blessed in their children if they become rich, if
they marry wealth, if they strike out into profitable enterprises
in trade, or if they attain eminence in the profession which
they have espoused. Their parents will go to their beds
rejoicing and awake perfectly satisfied, though their boys are
hastening down to Hell, if they are also making money by the
bushel. They have no greater joy than that their children are
having their portion in this life and laying up treasure where
rust corrupts it. Though neither their sons nor daughters
show any signs of the new birth, give no evidence of being rich
towards God, manifest no traces of electing love or redeeming
Grace or the regenerating power of the Holy Spirit, yet there
are parents who are content with their condition.
    Now I can only say of such professing parents that they
have need to question whether *they* are Christians, and if
they will not question it themselves, they must give some of
us leave to hold it in serious debate. When a man's heart is
really right with God and he, himself, has been saved from
the wrath to come and is living in the light of his heavenly
Father's countenance, it is certain that he is anxious about
his children's souls, prizes their immortal natures and feels
that nothing could give him greater joy than to hear that his
children walk in the Truth of God. Judge yourselves, then,
Beloved, this morning, by the gentle but searching test of the
text.
    If you are professing Christians, but cannot say that you
have no greater joy than the conversion of your children, you
have reason to question whether you ought to have made such
a profession at all! (Ibid.; emphasis in original)

People cannot see your heart, but they can see your life. Walk, live out, day by day, the gospel truth that is in you by virtue of your union with Christ. Abide in Christ and bear much fruit (cf. John 15).

Serve Faithfully (3 John 5-6)

John commends Gaius, "Dear friend, you are showing faithfulness." What was he doing? It seems he was showing hospitality and entertaining brothers, traveling missionaries for Jesus sent from John. These were strangers, persons he did not know. John knew of Gaius's service because on their return to John "they testified" of his love "in front of the church." John responds by encouraging him to "just keep on doing what you are doing" (paraphrase of v. 6). "Please keep up the good work" is the idea. In providing lodging, food, money, encouragement, and prayer, and in standing with them even though they were "strangers," Gaius had honored God, the gospel, and John. Sensitive to the hospitality expectations of the ancient Near Eastern world, Gaius had received these traveling teachers into his home and honored the Lord and the apostle who sent them. His faithful service stands in striking contrast to the inhospitable Diotrephes, whom we meet in verses 9-10.

Minister Generously (3 John 7-8)

These verses provide three reasons we should help those whom God has called and sent out. First, they "set out for the sake of the Name" (i.e., the name of Jesus; cf. 1 John 2:12; Acts 4:12; 5:40-41; 9:16; 15:26; 21:13; Phil 2:9). This is the only mention of the Lord Jesus in 3 John. It is His Name we take to the nations. It is His gospel we proclaim. There is no other. Second, they were "accepting nothing from pagans," that is, unbelievers (Jew and Gentile alike). They did not attempt to finance God's work with the world's money. They depended, and rightly so, on the generosity and gifts of the church. In so doing they avoided the scandal of other traveling teachers who prided themselves in fleecing the countryside. Third, John wrote that "we ought to support such men so that we can be coworkers with the truth." We may not physically go where they go, but we can go with them anyway by our support. All pray. All give support. Some are sent. All are essential as we cooperate together in the work of God. It is well said, "There is no limit to how much good you can do if you do not care who gets the credit." God, multiply the sent. God, multiply the supporters.

Diotrephes: A Man with a Harmful Agenda
3 JOHN 9-10

Third John now takes a surprising and unexpected turn. If Gaius had the right balance, a man by the name of Diotrephes did not. He was basically Gaius's alter-ego at every turn, a man with a harmful and destructive agenda. The bottom line for Diotrephes was that he wanted to be the "boss" in the church. He loved himself and not others. With perverted ambition and a dominating spirit, he opposed the apostle John and set himself up as lord in the church. If anyone took exception to his actions, that person was censured and dismissed from the congregation. Carnality personified, Diotrephes is mirrored today by many in the church who exhibit a similar lust for power. They are leaders who have a messiah complex. They have taken their eyes off of Jesus and forgotten that He, and He alone, is Lord and Savior.

Just as John commended Gaius in four areas, he condemned Diotrephes in four areas. His stern rebukes are instructive for us all.

Do Not Be Driven by Prideful Ambition (3 John 9)

John wrote a letter that is now lost to us (v. 9). It was probably a letter of commendation for the missionaries. Its reception met a problem in the person of Diotrephes, who is mentioned only here in the New Testament. He "loves to have first place among them." The issue here was not a doctrinal problem but personal pride. He loved being first, number one, the captain of the ship, the CEO, the center of attention, and the main attraction. Colossians 1:18 says only Jesus is "to have first place in everything." Amazingly, Diotrephes took for himself the position only Jesus should hold. Tragically, many today take for themselves the position only Jesus should hold. It may be a pastor, minister of worship or students, a deacon, a prominent layman, or a powerful and influential family. We do not know who Diotrephes was. We do know he was driven by prideful ambition.

Do Not Display Pompous Arrogance (3 John 9)

Diotrephes would not "receive" John and his missionaries. Incredibly he felt the apostle had nothing to offer, nothing he or the church needed. John was old news. It was time for him to retire and move off the scene. Such arrogance would have been culturally shameful. It is spiritually shocking. Imagine you had a chance today to hear the apostle John.

Would you say, "We don't need to hear anything he has to say!"? Of
course not! But here the older, wiser apostle was being "kicked to the
curb." The arrogance of this behavior takes your breath away.

Do Not Deliver Perverse Accusations (3 John 10)

John did not fear personal and public confrontation when a situation
demanded it (v. 10). If he comes, and the implication is he will (v. 14),
he will confront Diotrephes, beginning with his perverse accusations
(cf. 1 Tim 5:20). Diotrephes was "slandering . . . with malicious words."
He was talking trash, "gossiping maliciously" (NIV). With vicious and
wicked intent, Diotrephes had lied about John and slandered him.
Trying to stack the deck and win the day, he would stop at nothing to
get his way, even if it meant lying and acting with a heavy hand.

Do Not Dominate with Profane Activity (3 John 10)

There is a sick, sad digression to Diotrephes' behavior. Do you see it?
Ambition led to *arrogance*, which then led to *accusations*, culminating in
actions. He acted exactly the opposite of Gaius, but then he went further.
He slandered John, gave a cold shoulder to these missionaries from
John, stopped others who would have received them, and kicked out of
the church anyone who attempted to help them—all because he loved
himself and loved his agenda, and he had to have his own way no matter
what (v. 10b).

In a somewhat funny but all too tragic comment, the great Greek
scholar A. T. Robertson wrote, "some . . . years ago I wrote an article
on Diotrephes for a denominational paper. The editor told me that
25 deacons stopped the paper to show their resentment against being
personally attacked in the paper" (*Word Pictures*, vol. 6, 263). Of course
Robertson had mentioned no one by name!

Prideful ambition, pompous arrogance, perverse accusations, and
profane activity are all very real dangers for Christians and church
leaders. Therefore, we must watch our motives, watch our decisions,
watch our tongues, and watch our actions.

Demetrius: A Man with a Good Testimony
3 JOHN 11-12

In a wise rhetorical strategy, John sandwiches evil Diotrephes between
godly Gaius and a good man named Demetrius. A man like Diotrephes

can be impressive, build a following, and gather supporters who admire or even idolize him. John was aware of this. He knew we all imitate someone. Be careful whom you admire. Make sure it is someone like Gaius or someone like Demetrius (v. 12).

Pursue a Godly Example (3 John 11)

After calling Gaius "dear friend" for a fourth time. John says in verse 11, "Do not imitate what is evil, but what is good." This command is a present imperative. It is a word calling for continuous action. The word "imitate" is related to our word "mimic." Why imitate or mimic one ("the good") and not the other ("the bad")? Simply put, it gives evidence to whom you belong. You see, "the one who does good is of God" (v. 11). He gives tangible evidence that he belongs to God. In contrast, the one whose life is characterized by evil gives evidence that he is lost, that he "has not seen God." B. F. Wescott said, "He who does good proves by his action that his life springs from God" (*The Epistles of St. John*, 241).

Ultimately we should imitate Jesus (1 Cor 11:1). He is our supreme example who will never fail us (Heb 12:2-3). However, we need earthly, everyday examples to imitate as well. We need men and women to whom we can point our sons and daughters, our boys and girls, and say, "Go and live like him; go and be like her." We should strive to be such examples. So, be careful whom you watch, and be mindful of who watches you!

Possess a Good Testimony (3 John 12)

Demetrius probably brought this letter to Gaius. The letter would also serve as his recommendation from John. A threefold witness is put forward to commend him (v. 12; cf. Deut 17:6; 19:15). He has a good testimony (or witness) from *everyone*, from *the truth itself*, and from *John and his community.*

Over time, people have watched this man Demetrius and found him to be a man of integrity and godliness. Like Gaius, what he believed and lived were beautifully balanced. It is doubtful everyone agreed with Demetrius's commitment to Christ and Christian truth, but his life was above reproach and beyond question. He walked with God, studied His Word, loved Jesus, and loved people—both saved and lost. Here was a man I could point my sons to and say, "Be like him." Could I also point them to you? Could you point your children to me?

John: A Man with a Pastor's Heart
3 JOHN 13-14

Throughout this letter John, through positive and negative examples, has painted a portrait of good, godly leadership. He has shown us the balance of belief and behavior that is necessary if we are to be faithful witnesses for King Jesus. He has revealed his pastor's heart. As he brings this letter to a close, that heart of love and compassion continues to shine brightly.

Desire the Presence of Fellow Believers (3 John 13)

With a full and burdened heart, John longs to come and visit Gaius and his friends. He will embrace Gaius, and he will confront Diotrephes. Pen and ink are nice, but they are not enough. John wanted to see them. Similarly in our own day, talk of online cyber churches sounds intriguing, but they can never be a substitute for a personal touch.

Desire Peace for Fellow Believers (3 John 14)

John hoped to see them soon. He could hardly wait until later. He wanted a face-to-face (literally, a "mouth to mouth"), up-close and personal time together. A letter, e-mail, or text message is a poor substitute for personal interaction.

He closed with an expression of "peace" (cf. Rom 5:1; Phil 4:7), something the Diotrephes affair had robbed them of. To accentuate that blessing, John told Gaius that "the friends send you greetings." They knew the situation with Diotrephes and they stood with John. This is the only place in the New Testament that believers are called friends, perhaps reflecting John 15:13 where Jesus says, "No one has greater love than this, that someone would lay down his life for his friends."

Finally, John asked Gaius to say hello to everyone, one by one, name by name. Like John, who reflected the heart of the God who saves us one by one, we too should love and care in the same manner: one by one. To do so is to cultivate a good reputation. To do so is to live a life that brings praise to the name of Jesus.

Reflect and Discuss

1. Which of these men do you identify with? Which provides the most needed corrective for your life?
2. Why is reputation important for the Christian? What are some dangers of becoming too concerned with reputation?
3. What would happen if God blessed you physically to the same degree as your spiritual health? What areas of concern could you identify?
4. Why is John so joyful in Gaius's faithfulness? What is the source of your joy? Is it connected to the spiritual fruitfulness of other Christians?
5. How can you invest in others so that you might see their spiritual fruit and find joy in them? Who has God placed in your life for you to invest in as a spiritual child?
6. How do you show the love of Christ to strangers? Why is it more difficult to love people we don't know?
7. How can you work to support faithful ministers of the gospel? Who are you partnering with for the spread of Jesus' name?
8. Why is pride such a danger in the Christian life? Why is it especially hard for church leaders? How can you work to combat pride in your life and ministry?
9. How can those who aren't pastors imitate John's pastoral heart? What in his character is commendable to all?
10. Why is being physically present with other believers important to John? How might this desire translate to the church in the digital age?

WORKS CITED

Anonymous. *Embracing Obscurity: Becoming Nothing in Light of God's Everything*. Nashville: B&H, 2012.

Anyabwile, Thabiti. Unpublished sermon manuscript.

Akin, Daniel L. *1, 2, 3 John*. New American Commentary, vol. 38. Nashville: B&H, 2001.

Ash, Lorraine. "Bishop Will Retire But He Won't Stop." *Daily Record*, January 27, 2000.

Augustine. *The Enchiridion on Faith, Hope and Love*. Washington, D.C.: Regnery, 1961.

———. *Homilies on the Gospel According to S. John and His First Epistle*, vol. 2. Oxford: James Parker, 1880.

———. *On Christian Doctrine*. In *The Works of Aurelius Augustine, Bishop of Hippo: A New Translation*, vol. 9. Edited by Marcus Dods. Translated by J. F. Shaw. Edinburgh: T&T Clark, 1892.

———. *Saint Augustine's Confessions*. Lafayette, IN: Sovereign Grace, 2001.

Begg, Alistair. "A Word of Warning." Sermon preached at Parkside Church on April 1, 1990. Accessed February 10, 2014. http://www.truthforlife.org/resources/sermon/a-word-of-warning.

Beilby, James K., and Paul Rhodes Eddy. "The Quest for the Historical Jesus: An Introduction." In *The Historical Jesus: Five Views*. Edited by James K. Beilby and Paul Rhodes Eddy. Downers Grove: IVP Academic, 2009.

Boice, James Montgomery. *The Epistles of John*. Grand Rapids, MI: Zondervan, 1979.

Bonhoeffer, Dietrich. *The Collected Sermons of Dietrich Bonhoeffer*. Translated by Douglas W. Stott, Anne Schmidt-Lange, Isabel Best, Scott A. Moore, and Claudia D. Bergmann. Minneapolis: Fortress Press, 2012.

Bridges, Jerry. *Transforming Grace*. Colorado Springs, CO: Nav Press, 2008.

Bruce, F. F. *The Epistles of John*. London: Old Tappan, 1970.

Calvin, John. *Institutes of the Christian Religion*, vol. 1. Edited by John T. McNeill. Translated by Ford Lewis Battles. Louisville, KY: Westminster John Knox, 1960.

Chalke, Steve, and Alan Mann. *The Lost Message of Jesus*. Grand Rapids: Zondervan, 2004.

Clayton, Norman John. "Now I Belong to Jesus." Copyright © 1938, 1943 Norman J. Clayton. Renewed 1966, 1971 Wordspring Music, LLC (Admin. by Word Music Group, Inc.) — CCLI 17638.

Colson, Charles. *Loving God*. Grand Rapids: Zondervan, 1983.

Cook, Fredrick Charles, editor. *The Holy Bible, Authorized Version, with Commentary and a Revision of the Translation by Bishops and Other Clergy of the Anglican Church*, New Testament, Volume IV. London: John Murray, 1881.

Driscoll, Mark. *1, 2, and 3 John: Walking in the Light*. Mars Hill Sermon and Study Series. Accessed April 3, 2014. http://cdn.marshill.com/files/collection/documents/epistles-of-john_9082_document.pdf, 18-19.

Driscoll, Mark, and Gerry Breshears. *Death by Love: Letters from the Cross*. Wheaton, IL: Crossway, 2008.

Dostoevsky, Fyodor. *The Brothers Karamazov*. Translated by Constance Garnett. 1880; repr., New York: Modern Library, 1996.

Edwards, Jonathan. *Some Thoughts Concerning the Present Revival of Religion in New England*. In Vol. 1 of *The Works of Jonathan Edwards*. Edited by E. Hickman. Carlisle, PA: Banner of Truth Trust, 1995.

Edwards, Jonathan, and John Angell James. "Growth in Grace." Pages 35–62 in *A Casket of Four Jewels: For Young Christians*. Boston: Gould, Kendall, & Lincoln, 1844.

Foster, Richard J. *Celebration of Discipline: The Path to Spiritual Growth*. San Francisco: Harper & Row, 1978.

Franklin, Benjamin. "Letter to Ezra Stiles." Accessed Feb. 10, 2014. http://www.constitution.org/primarysources/franklin-stiles.html.

Funk, Robert W. *The Acts of Jesus: What Did Jesus Really Do?* Salem, OR: Polebridge, 1998.

Gordon, M. R. "Regeneration." Pages 1005–6 in *New Bible Dictionary*, 3rd ed. Edited by I. Howard Marshall, A. R. Millard, J. I. Packer, and D. J. Wiseman. Downers Grove, IL: InterVarsity, 1996.

Hannah. "C T Studd: 2 Dec 1860–16 July 1931." Accessed February 10, 2014. http://wycliffe.org.uk/blog/2011/07/c-t-studd-2-dec-1860-16-july-1931.

Hick, John. *The Metaphor of God Incarnate: Christology in a Pluralistic Age.* Louisville: Westminster John Knox Press, 1993.

Hiebert, D. Edmond. "An Exposition of 1 John 4:7-21." *Bibliotheca Sacra* 147, no. 585 (January–March 1990).

———. "An Exposition of 1 John 5:13-21." *Bibliotheca Sacra* 147, no. 587 (July–September 1990).

Holmes, Arthur F. *All Truth Is God's Truth.* Grand Rapids: Eerdmans, 1977.

Keller, Timothy J. "Preaching the Gospel in a Post-Modern World." Reformed Theological Seminary Class Notes, January 2002. Accessed July 8, 2013. http://www.eucatastrophe.com/blog/wp-content/uploads/2006/12/keller-on-preaching-syllabus.pdf.

———. "Keller on Preaching to a Post-Modern City II: Preaching to Create Spiritually Inclusive Worship." Accessed July 8, 2013. http://www.redeemer2.com/themovement/issues/2004/august/postmoderncity_2_p3.html.

———. "Talking about Idolatry in a Postmodern Age." Accessed July 8, 2013. http://www.monergism.com/postmodernidols.html.

Lewis, C. S. *Mere Christianity.* London: Collins, 1952.

Linne, Shai. "Fal$e Teacher$." On the album *Lyrical Theology Part 1: Theology.* Philadelphia: Lamp Mode Recordings, 2013.

"'Love' as Seen by Frank Pittman and a Bunch of Kids," *Smart Marriages,* March 12, 2002. Accessed February 10, 2014. http://lists101.his.com/pipermail/smartmarriages/2002-March/001032.html.

Luther, Martin. *What Luther Says: An Anthology.* Vol. 1. Translated by Ewald M. Plas. St. Louis: Concordia, 1959.

———. "Preface to Galatians." In vol. 27 of *Luther's Works.* Edited by J. Pelikan. Saint Louis: Concordia, 1964.

———. *Treatise on Good Works.* Vol. 44 of *Luther's Works.* Translated by W. A. Lambert. Revised and edited by James Atkinson. Philadelphia: Fortress Press, 1966.

———. *Lectures on the First Epistle of John.* Vol. 30 of *Luther's Works.* Edited by J. Pelikan. Translated by W. A. Hansen. St. Louis: Concordia, 1967.

MacArthur, John. *1–3 John.* Chicago: Moody Publishers, 2007.

Macquarrie, John. *Jesus Christ in Modern Thought*. Philadelphia: Trinity Press International, 1990.

Marshall, I. Howard. *The Epistles of John*. New International Commentary on the New Testament. Grand Rapids: Wm. B. Eerdmans, 1978.

McCoy, Colt, and Matt Carter. *The Real Win: A Man's Quest for Authentic Success*. Colorado Springs: Multnomah Books, 2013.

Menninger, Karl. *Whatever Became of Sin?* New York: Hawthorn Books: 1973.

Merkle, Benjamin L. "What Is the Meaning of 'Idols' in 1 John 5:21?" *Bibliotheca Sacra* 169, no. 675 (July–September 2012).

Merritt, James. "Do You Know For Sure." Unpublished sermon notes.

Muggeridge, Malcolm. *Seeing through the Eye: Malcolm Muggeridge on Faith*. Edited by Cecil Kuhne. San Francisco: Ignatius Press, 2005.

Newbigin, Lesslie. *The Gospel in a Pluralist Society*. Grand Rapids, MI: Wm. B. Eerdmans, 1989.

Pascal, Blaise. *Pascal's Pensées*. New York: E. P. Dutton, 1958.

Plummer, A. *The Epistles of St. John*. Cambridge: The University Press, 1900.

Piper, John. "The Son of God Appeared to Destroy the Works of the Devil," sermon preached at Bethlehem Baptist Church on December 23, 1984. Accessed February 10, 2014. http://www.desiringgod.org/resource-library/sermons/the-son-of-god-appeared-to-destroy-the-works-of-the-devil.

———. "Eternal Life Has Appeared in Christ." Sermon preached at Bethlehem Baptist Church on January 27, 1985. Accessed February 10, 2014. http://www.desiringgod.org/resource-library/sermons/eternal-life-has-appeared-in-christ.

———. "The One Who Loves Lives in Light." Sermon preached at Bethlehem Baptist Church on February 24, 1985. Accessed February 10, 2014. http://www.desiringgod.org/resource-library/sermons/the-one-who-loves-lives-in-light.

———. "The Strong Need Strength." Sermon preached at Bethlehem Baptist Church on March 3, 1985. Accessed February 10, 2014. http://www.desiringgod.org/resource-library/sermons/the-strong-need-strength.

———. "Test the Spirits to See Whether They Are of God." Sermon preached at Bethlehem Baptist Church on May 5, 1985. Accessed February 10, 2014. http://www.desiringgod.org/resource-library/sermons/test-the-spirits-to-see-whether-they-are-of-god.

———. "Love One Another for Love Is of God." Sermon preached at Bethlehem Baptist Church on May 12, 1985. Accessed February 10, 2014. http://www.desiringgod.org/resource-library/sermons/love-one-another-for-love-is-of-god.

———. "The Word of God Abides in You, and You Have Overcome the Evil One." Sermon preached at Bethlehem Baptist Church on January 7, 2007. Accessed February 10, 2014. http://www.desiringgod.org/resource-library/sermons/the-word-of-god-abides-in-you-and-you-have-overcome-the-evil-one.

———. "Everyone Who Has Been Born of God Overcomes the World." Sermon preached at Bethlehem Baptist Church on February 24, 2008. Accessed February 10, 2014. http://www.desiringgod.org/resource-library/sermons/everyone-who-has-been-born-of-god-overcomes-the-world.

———. "Regeneration, Faith, Love: In That Order." Sermon preached at Bethlehem Baptist Church on March 2, 2008. Accessed February 10, 2014. http://www.desiringgod.org/resource-library/sermons/regeneration-faith-love-in-that-order.

———. "The New Birth Produces Love." Sermon preached at Bethlehem Baptist Church on March 16, 2008. Accessed February 10, 2014. http://www.desiringgod.org/resource-library/sermons/the-new-birth-produces-love.

Powlison, David. "The Therapeutic Gospel." *IX Marks eJournal* 4, no. 5 (July–August 2007). Accessed February 10, 2014. http://www.9marks.org/files/ejournal200745julaug.pdf.

Robertson, Archibald Thomas. *Word Pictures in the New Testament.* Vol. 6. Nashville: Broadman, 1933.

Rodgers, Adrian. *Adrianisms, Volume Two: The Wit and Wisdom of Adrian Rodgers.* Memphis: Love Worth Finding Ministries, 2007.

Rosten, Leo. "Bertrand Russell and God: A Memoir." *The Saturday Review,* Feb. 23, 1974.

Schaff, Philip. *Nicene and Post-Nicene Fathers.* Series II, volume 4. Accessed Feb. 11, 2014. http://www.ccel.org/ccel/schaff/npnf204.

Schleiermacher, Friedrich. *The Christian Faith.* Edited and translated by H. R. Mackintosh and J. S. Stewart. Edinburgh: T&T Clark, 1956.

Sills, Michael. *The Missionary Call: Find Your Place in God's Plan for the World.* Chicago: Moody, 2008.

Spurgeon, Charles Haddon. "Faith and Regeneration." Sermon preached at the Metropolitan Tabernacle on March 5, 1871.

Accessed February 10, 2014. http://www.spurgeongems.org/vols16-18/chs979.pdf.

———. "The Conditions of Power in Prayer." Sermon preached at the Metropolitan Tabernacle on March 23, 1873. Accessed February 10, 2014. http://www.spurgeongems.org/vols19-21/chs1103.pdf.

———. "The Parent's and Pastor's Joy." Sermon preached at the Metropolitan Tabernacle on December 21, 1873. Accessed February 10, 2014. http://www.spurgeongems.org/vols19-21/chs1148.pdf.

———. "The Three Witnesses." Sermon preached at the Metropolitan Tabernacle on August 9, 1874. Accessed February 10, 2014. http://www.spurgeongems.org/vols19-21/chs1187.pdf.

———. "Honest Dealings with God." Sermon preached at the Metropolitan Tabernacle on June 20, 1875. Accessed February 10, 2014. http://www.spurgeongems.org/vols19-21/chs1241.pdf.

———. "The Priest Dispensed With." Sermon preached at the Metropolitan Tabernacle on August 15, 1875. Accessed February 10, 2014. http://www.spurgeongems.org/vols19-21/chs1250.pdf.

———. "Faith, and the Witness Upon Which It Is Founded." Sermon preached at the Metropolitan Tabernacle, n.d. Accessed February 10, 2014. http://www.spurgeongems.org/vols19-21/chs1213.pdf.

———. *An All-Round Ministry.* Carlisle, PA: Banner of Truth, 1960.

Storms, Sam. "First John 4:7-21" Enjoying God Ministries, posted November 5, 2006. Accessed February 10, 2014. http://www.samstorms.com/all-articles/post/first-john-4:7-21.

———. "First John 2:28–3:3." Enjoying God Ministries, posted November 10, 2006. Accessed February 10, 2014. http://www.samstorms.com/all-articles/post/first-john-2:28–3:3.

Stott, John R. W. *The Cross of Christ.* Downers Grove, IL: Intervarsity Press, 1986.

———. *The Letters of John: An Introduction and Commentary.* 2nd ed. Grand Rapids: Wm. B. Eerdmans, 1988.

Strode, Tom. "China: 336 Million Abortions in Barely 4 Decades." *Baptist Press*, March 19, 2013. Online: http://www.bpnews.net/bpnews.asp?id=39913. Accessed February 10, 2014.

Tchividjian, Tullian. *Jesus + Nothing = Everything.* Wheaton: Crossway, 2011.

Thomas, Scott, and Tom Wood. *Gospel Coach: Shepherding Leaders to Glorify God.* Grand Rapids, MI: Zondervan, 2012.

Torrey, R. A. *The Power of Prayer and the Prayer of Power.* New York: Fleming H. Revell Company, 1924.

Tozer, A. W. *The Pursuit of God.* Camp Hill, PA: Christian Publications, 2000.

Vaughan, Curtis. *1, 2, 3 John: A Study Guide.* Grand Rapids, MI: Zondervan, 1970.

Walker, James. Personal correspondence.

Warfield, B. B. *The Person and Work of Christ.* Philadelphia: Presbyterian and Reformed Publishing, 1950.

Westcott, Brooke Foss. *The Epistles of St. John: The Greek Text with Notes and Essays.* Grand Rapids, MI: Wm. B. Eerdmans, 1955.

White, James Emery. *The Church in an Age of Crisis: 25 New Realities Facing Christianity.* Grand Rapids, MI: Baker, 2012.

Wiersbe, Warren W. *Be Real.* Wheaton, IL: Victor Books, 1972.

Williams, Delores S. "Re-Imagining Jesus," *1993 Re-imagining Conference Audiotapes.* Apple Valley, MN: Resource Express, 1993.

———. *Sisters in the Wilderness: The Challenge of Womanist God-Talk.* Maryknoll, NY: Orbis Books, 1993.

Woodward, Kenneth L. "The Way the World Ends." *Newsweek,* November 1, 1999.

Zacharias, Ravi. *Can Man Live Without God.* Dallas: Word, 1994.

SCRIPTURE INDEX